WHY I WROTE THIS BOOK

It happens everywhere I go.

I have spoken in 39 countries during the past 31 years I have traveled as a teacher. When I finish speaking on the principles of prosperity, and the possibility of the Seed-faith lifestyle, someone always questions me.

"I've been giving and giving and giving for years. I never receive my Harvests. These wonderful things I hear about never really happen to me. Why? This doesn't seem to work for me." Their countenance shows sincerity. Obviously, I could give an immediate answer that would be scriptural, accurate and revolutionary. But, time never permits in the rush of my hectic schedule. Also, I often see so much pain and agony on their faces that I feel my brief or concise answer would be misinterpreted or simplistic. It would appear uncaring and incomplete. Nothing could be further from the truth.

I do care. Deeply.

You see, poverty has been the tragic thread through the garments of my own background. I understand and totally despise every kind of lack.

Poverty does not help anyone. Millions are starving to death daily on this incredible and blessed planet. Fathers are angry with themselves for unproductive lives. Mothers are frustrated, clinging desperately to their children they have labored to bring into this world. Dreams are being aborted every moment.

The tragedy is that poverty is unnecessary.

You see, God is a miracle God. He is a magnificent provider. He is a heavenly Father Who truly cares for us.

God is the magnificent Giver of every good gift. "If ye then, being evil, know how to give good gifts unto your children, how much more shall your Father which is in heaven give good things to them that ask Him?" (Matthew 7:11).

God has promised to be Your Provider. "Wherefore, if God so clothe the grass of the field which to day is, and to morrow is cast into the oven, shall He not much more clothe you, O ye of little faith?" (Matthew 6:30).

Prosperity is the most controversial subject today in Christianity. Why is it? *Ignorance.* There is unbelievable ignorance about its *purpose* on the earth. You see, its purpose is to *help you complete your Assignment on earth.*

Many are ignorant about the *principles that produce* prosperity. That also is easy to answer. Money is merely a reward for solving a problem. *When you solve problems for others, you generate money.*

Many are ignorant about the Source of financial blessing — your heavenly Father. Many are ignorant about the Master Key to Financial Prosperity — the Master Key of Wisdom. "Riches and honour are with Me; yea, durable riches and righteousness. That I may cause those that love Me to inherit substance; and I will fill their treasures" (Proverbs 8:18, 21).

When you increase your Wisdom, you will increase your wealth. "Length of days is in her right hand; and in her left hand riches and honour"

31 REAON

PEOPLE DO NOT RECEIVE THEIR

FINANCIAL HARVE$T

MIKE MURDOCK

Unless otherwise indicated, all Scripture quotations are taken from the King James Version of the Bible.

31 Reasons People Do Not Receive Their Financial Harvest
ISBN 1-56394-057-4
Copyright © 1997 by *MIKE MURDOCK*
All publishing rights belong exclusively to Wisdom International
Published by The Wisdom Center
4051 Denton Highway • Fort Worth, Texas 76117
1-888-WISDOM-1 (1-817-759-0300)
Website: www.TheWisdomCenter.TV

(Proverbs 3:16). Wisdom produces financial blessing. "Blessed is the man that feareth the Lord, wealth and riches shall be in his house: and his righteousness endureth for ever" (Psalm 112:1, 3). The confusion is unnecessary.

The only cure for confusion is the Wisdom of God. You can simply ask, and He has promised to give it to you. "If any of you lack Wisdom, let him ask of God, that giveth to all men liberally, and upbraideth not; and it shall be given him" (James 1:5).

Every parent needs money. "But if any provide not for his own, and especially for those of his own house, he hath denied the faith, and is worse than an infidel" (1 Timothy 5:8). "If ye then, being evil, know how to give good gifts unto your children, how much more shall your Father which is in heaven give good things to them that ask Him?" (Matthew 7:11).

Every minister is worthy of abundant finances. "Let the elders that rule well be counted worthy of double honour, especially they who labour in the word and doctrine. For the scripture sayeth, Thou shalt not muzzle the ox that treadeth out the corn. And, the labourer is worthy of his reward" (1 Timothy 5:17-18).

Hypocrisy abounds. It seems highly acceptable to be wealthy, yet unacceptable for Christians to discuss it. This kind of hypocrisy is cancerous. Pharisees are still among us. Slinging accusations and cries of "materialistic," they stride across the stage of mocked discipleship, making the *appearance* of sacrifice. Many others who have been broken and torn apart by financial losses, stare confused with envious eyes and jealous hearts at those who are sitting at the Table of Plenty. Still others, trying to justify their lack and losses, insist that prosperity is a matter of the *sovereignty of God* — something He alone decides without the participation of men. If Prosperity is the sovereignty of God there is neither reward for Wisdom nor penalty for ignorance.

This *must* change.

Controversy is the child of ignorance. That's why the Word of God is so important in your daily life as a *continuous* powerful influence.

You can be *debt free.*

You can drive back the darkness of financial poverty.

You can unlock the Golden Windows of Heaven so the River of Plenty can flow down into your own home, into your children, through your home church, through the hands of missionaries and ministers who are healing the broken in this generation.

Every ministry needs financial blessing. The missing weapon between the church and the evangelization of the world is *money.*

Yet almost nobody realizes it.

When you hear ministers speak, they blame those in the pew for failure to witness. Missionaries blame unconcerned churches. Others blame satan, demons or lazy Christians.

Yet, one single preacher can reach ten million souls in a single night of television. Then, why isn't everyone hearing the gospel continuously? Financial needs. As God blesses, it will become possible to purchase more television stations, radio stations, and print billions of pieces of literature that will shake this world for God. Money buys television stations. Money purchases radio stations. Money puts vehicles, supplies and books in the hands of missionaries throughout the earth.

The only weapon that satan seems helpless against is the weapon of financial Harvest. That's why he has targeted every demon to *stop the tongue of those who teach financial prosperity to the Body of Christ.*

He will fail. Satan cannot succeed. It is only a matter of time for the revelation of God on financial blessing will rise victorious among the people of God in this generation.

Your fountain of wisdom is already flowing. How do I know? You have chosen to read this book. This reveals your pursuit, hunger, and recognition of the Wisdom of God.

You will never be the same again after reading this book. Here is your own Prosperity Handbook for your family. *"Thirty-One Reasons"* can be read daily. Choose a different chapter each morning. *Read it aloud* at the breakfast table. *Keep your Bible handy* to confirm any Scripture the Holy Spirit might bring to your remembrance.

Too many people are *hurting.*

Too many people are *hungry.*

Too many people are *ignorant.*

Too many people are *poor.*

Tragically, it is totally unnecessary. Prosperity is having enough Divine Provision to complete a Divine Assignment.

You *can* prosper.

You *must* prosper.

You *will* prosper.

> *That's why I wrote this book.*
> -MIKE MURDOCK

CONTENTS

REASON   PAGE

1   MANY DO NOT REALLY BELIEVE THAT GOD   13
     WANTS THEM TO PROSPER FINANCIALLY.

2   MANY PEOPLE NEVER DREAM BIG ENOUGH   21
     TO REQUIRE A FINANCIAL MIRACLE.

3   SOME PEOPLE BELIEVE THEIR FINANCIAL   27
     INCOME DEPENDS ON THEIR BOSS OR
     LOVED ONES.

4   MANY DO NOT REALLY RESPECT MONEY   31
     AND DO NOT RECOGNIZE IT AS A WEAPON
     AND TOOL FOR GOOD.

5   SOME PEOPLE NEVER EVEN ASK FOR A   39
     SPECIFIC AND SIGNIFICANT FINANCIAL
     HARVEST.

6   SOME DO NOT REALLY BELIEVE THAT   47
     THEY DESERVE A FINANCIAL HARVEST.

7   MANY RELY UPON THEIR OWN ABILITIES   57
     INSTEAD OF THE SUPERNATURAL POWER
     OF GOD.

8   MANY NEVER FULLY GRASP THE IMPACT,   61
     INFLUENCE AND MIRACLES THAT AN
     UNCOMMON HARVEST COULD PRODUCE
     FOR OTHERS.

Reason		Page
9	Many Do Not Recognize The Seed Or The Soil When They See It.	67
10	Many People Do Not Recognize A Harvest When It Does Arrive.	75
11	Some Give Only When They Feel Like It Instead Of When A Man Of God Inspires Them.	85
12	Many Are Not Working At Their Place Of Assignment.	91
13	Most People Have Never Learned The Secret Of Giving Their Seed A Specific Assignment.	103
14	Many Forget Or Refuse To Pay Their Vows Made To God.	109
15	Many Are Unwilling To Patiently Sit At The Feet Of A Financial Mentor.	115
16	Many Have Never Been Taught To Sow With An Expectation Of A Return.	127
17	Many Do Not Pursue A Harvest, Because They Have Not Yet Tasted The Pain Of Poverty.	133

REASON   PAGE

18   MILLIONS STEAL THE TITHE, THE HOLY   141
      PORTION GOD RESERVED FOR HIMSELF.

19   MANY REFUSE TO SOW DURING TIMES   149
      OF CRISIS.

20   SOME REFUSE TO WAIT LONG ENOUGH   153
      FOR THEIR HARVEST.

21   MILLIONS REFUSE TO OBEY THE VERY   161
      BASIC AND SIMPLE LAWS OF GOD.

22   THOUSANDS ARE UNWILLING TO START   169
      THEIR HARVEST WITH A SMALL SEED.

23   SOME DO NOT KNOW THE DIFFERENCE   175
      BETWEEN GOOD SOIL AND BAD SOIL.

24   SOME REFUSE TO SOW CONSISTENTLY.   181

25   MILLIONS ARE UNTHANKFUL AND DO   189
      NOT APPRECIATE WHAT GOD HAS
      ALREADY GIVEN TO THEM.

26   MOST PEOPLE FAIL TO RECOGNIZE THE   197
      ENEMIES OF THEIR HARVEST AND
      PROSPERITY.

27   MILLIONS ARE NOT EXPERIENCING   205
      INCREASE BECAUSE NOBODY HAS YET
      TOLD THEM ABOUT THE PRINCIPLE OF
      SEED-FAITH.

Reason   Page

28   Many Are Too Proud To Even Admit   225
         That They Need A Harvest.

29   Some Rebel Against An Instruction   229
         From A Financial Deliverer God Has
         Anointed To Unlock Their Faith
         During Their Time Of Crisis.

30   Many Refuse To Sow Proportionate   237
         To The Harvest They Desire.

31   Millions Do Not Instantly Obey The   243
         Holy Spirit Without Negotiation.

≈ Psalm 84:11 ≈

"No good thing will He withhold from them
that walk uprightly."

∞ 1 ∞

Many Do Not Really Believe That God Wants Them To Prosper Financially.

Nobody Is More Misunderstood Than God.

Many believe that God is simply a spiritual force, a supreme being, "the Man upstairs."

They have not fully understood that He is "touched with the feeling of our infirmities" (Hebrews 4:15).

Yet, He invited us to approach Him boldly for every need in our life. "Let us therefore come boldly unto the throne of grace, that we may obtain mercy, and find grace to help in time of need" (Hebrews 4:16). Obviously, *you* must have the *sensitivity* to know *when* you need Him; the *humility* to pursue His mercy, and the *desperation* to come boldly to Him.

Someone once said that twenty percent of what Jesus talked about involved finances. He cared.

God wants you to have enough finances to provide everything your loved ones need for their success. "But if any provide not for his own, especially for those of his own house, he hath denied the faith, and is worse than an infidel" (1 Timothy 5:8).

God wants you to have enough finances to

provide an uncommon and wonderful income for your spiritual leaders and pastors. "Let the elders that rule well be counted worthy of double honour, especially they who labour in the word and doctrine. For the Scripture saith, Thou shalt not muzzle the ox that treadeth out the corn. And, the laborer is worthy of his reward" (1 Timothy 5:17, 18).

God wants you to have enough finances to send ministers throughout the world preaching the gospel. "And how shall they preach, except they be sent? as it is written, How beautiful are the feet of them that preach the gospel of peace, and bring glad tidings of good things!" (Romans 10:15).

God wants to provide enough finances for you to pay your taxes and obligations. "Render therefore unto Caesar the things which are Caesar's; and unto God the things that are God's" (Matthew 22:21).

God wants you to have enough finances to return the tithe back to His house that belongs to the work of God. "And all the tithe of the land, whether of the Seed of the land, or of the fruit of the tree, is the Lord's: it is holy unto the Lord" (Leviticus 27:30).

God wants you to have enough finances to give good and uncommon gifts to your children and those you love. "If ye then, being evil, know how to give good gifts unto your children, how much more shall your Father which is in heaven give good things to them that ask Him?" (Matthew 7:11).

God wants you to have enough finances to help the poor. "He that hath pity upon the poor lendeth unto the Lord; and that which he hath given will he pay him again" (Proverbs 19:17).

God wants you to have enough money to solve any emergency problem or crisis that arises. "Money answereth all things" (Ecclesiastes 10:19).

God wants to reveal to you where your financial provisions are located. He proved this to Elijah. "Turn thee eastward, and hide thyself by the brook Cherith, that is before Jordan... I have commanded the ravens to feed thee there" (1 Kings 17:3, 4).

God is concerned every time you have a financial crisis and will give you instructions to turn it around. He did it for Elijah. "And it came to pass after a while, that the brook dried up, because there had been no rain in the land. And the word of the Lord came unto him saying, Arise, get thee to Zarephath, which belongeth to Zidon, and dwell there:" (1 Kings 17:7-9).

God will give people instructions to help you in financial crisis. Again, He did it for the prophet Elijah, and He will do it for you! "Arise, and get thee to Zarephath, which belongeth to Zidon, and dwell there: behold, I have commanded a widow woman there to sustain thee" (1 Kings 17:9).

God always rewards holy conduct and behavior with financial provision. "No good thing will He withhold from them that walk uprightly" (Psalm 84:11).

God commanded everything He created to multiply and become more. "And God said, Let the earth bring forth grass, the herb yielding Seed, and the fruit tree yielding fruit after his kind, whose Seed is in itself, upon the earth... Let the waters bring forth abundantly the moving creature that hath life, and fowl that may fly above the earth... Be fruitful, and multiply, and fill the waters in the seas, and let fowl multiply in the earth..." (Genesis 1:11, 20, 22).

God commanded people to multiply and become

more. "Be fruitful, and multiply, and replenish the earth, and subdue it: and have dominion over the fish of the sea, and over the fowl of the air, and over every living thing that moveth upon the earth" (Genesis 1:28).

God even rewards productivity with more increase. Read the incredible story of the talents in Matthew 25. "Well done, good and faithful servant; thou hast been faithful over a few things, I will make thee ruler over many things: enter thou into the joy of thy Lord" (Matthew 25:23).

God punishes those who refuse to use their gifts and talents to become more. "Take therefore the talent from him, and give it unto him which hath ten talents... cast ye the unprofitable servant into outer darkness: there shall be weeping and gnashing of teeth" (Matthew 25:28-30).

God always promises financial blessing to those obedient to His instructions, laws and principles. "If thou shalt hearken diligently unto the voice of the Lord thy God, to observe and to do all His commandments which I command thee this day... all these blessings shall come on thee and overtake thee...The Lord shall command the blessing upon thee in thy storehouses...And the Lord shall make thee plenteous in goods...The Lord shall open unto thee His good treasure, the heaven to give the rain unto thy land in His season, and to bless all the work of thine hand: and thou shalt lend unto many nations, and thou shalt not borrow" (Deuteronomy 28:1-12).

God will teach you to profit, through mentors, the Holy Spirit and His Word. "Thus saith the Lord, thy redeemer, the Holy One of Israel; I am the Lord thy God which teacheth thee to profit, which leadeth thee by the way that thou shouldest go" (Isaiah 48:17).

So, become excited about your financial future. God cares. He has created a magnificent Financial Plan that *cannot fail* when you understand His heart.

You matter to Him.

Your *needs* matter to Him.

Every desire throbbing in your heart right this moment is vital and important to His heart. Your total prosperity is on His mind all the time.

God experiences great pleasure when you prosper financially. "Let the Lord be magnified, which hath pleasure in the prosperity of his servant" (Psalm 35:27).

Now, what is prosperity? It is far deeper than nice automobiles, beautiful diamonds, and money in

Prosperity Is Having Enough Of Divine Provision To Complete A Divine Assignment.

the bank. It is much greater than signing your signature on a huge loan that drains your family financially.

Prosperity is having enough of Divine Provision to complete a Divine Assignment.

God wants your journey through life to have sufficient energy, health and provision your entire journey. "Beloved, I wish above all things that thou mayest prosper and be in health, even as thy soul prospereth" (3 John 1:2).

God wants you to depend on Him as your total Source for every need in your life. "But thou shalt remember the Lord thy God: for it is He that giveth thee power to get wealth, that He may establish His covenant which He sware unto thy fathers, as it is this day" (Deuteronomy 8:18).

God is not poor. "The silver is mine, and the gold is mine, saith the Lord of hosts" (Haggai 2:8). "For every beast of the forest is mine, and the cattle upon a thousand hills" (Psalm 50:10).

When God saw a confused nation, He provided a Moses.

When Jesus saw the fear on the countenance of His disciples, He rebuked the wind.

When Jesus saw the hunger of the multitudes, He multiplied the fish and loaves.

Jesus Himself cursed the life of an unproductive fig tree. "And Jesus answered and said unto it, No man eat fruit of thee hereafter for ever...And in the morning, as they passed by, they saw the fig tree dried up from the roots" (Mark 11:14,20).

Jesus came to unlock a new level of provision and abundance in our life. "The thief cometh not, but for to steal, and to kill, and to destroy: I am come that they might have life, and that they might have it more abundantly" (John 10:10).

Jesus wanted you to know that the Father understood every single need you are experiencing. "Therefore take no thought, saying, What shall we eat? or, What shall we drink? or, Wherewithal shall we be clothed? For after all these things do the Gentiles seek: for your heavenly Father knoweth that you have need of all these things" (Matthew 6:31, 32).

Jesus taught that pursuit of righteousness, peace and joy in the Holy Spirit would be rewarded by financial blessing. "But seek ye first the kingdom of God, and His righteousness; and all these things shall be added unto you" (Matthew 6:33). "For the kingdom of God is not meat and drink: but righteousness, peace, and joy in the Holy Ghost" (Romans 14:17).

Jesus gave Peter instructions that brought finances to pay taxes. "Go thou to the sea, and cast an hook, and take up the fish that first cometh up; and when thou hast opened his mouth, thou shalt find a piece of money: that take, and give unto them for me and thee" (Matthew 17:27).

Jesus taught that attentiveness to details would increase and multiply your rewards. "Well done, good and faithful servant; thou hast been faithful over a few things, I will make thee ruler over many things" (Matthew 25:23).

Millions have not learned the alphabet, yet millions of others are reading and succeeding with their life.

Many have never traveled and met those of other nations, but the nations go right on succeeding and doing business.

So, you may not have understood this quality in the heart of God before, but, you do understand now. You cannot complain, gripe and blame others for your ignorance of the Principles of Prosperity from the heart of God. The Word of God is filled with examples of financial leaders such as Abraham, David, and Solomon. Their pursuit of God was rewarded in *every part* of their life.

Now, it is your turn for a financial turnaround and breakthrough.

Nobody else can do it for you.

Nobody else is responsible for it, but you.

You are not serving an uncaring, unfeeling God.

Your God truly cares about everything you need, especially the financial burden you are carrying today.

If you are not receiving a financial Harvest, evaluate again your understanding of your heavenly Father. Are you truly *discussing* your finances *with Him?* Did you discuss the *purchasing of your house?* Did you feel the *inner confirmation* of the Holy Spirit that the timing was accurate?

If you never discuss your major purchases, the problems you face on your job, and never bring the Holy Seed back to Him for multiplying, I doubt that you truly believe He is interested in the finances of your life.

You can change this today. Begin now. May I pray this special prayer for you?

"Heavenly Father, forgive us for not understanding Your heart when You've made it so plain and clear to us in Your Word. As we read the Scriptures, it is so evident to us that your heart is full of concern. You desire to impart Wisdom to us. Now, in the name of Jesus, we receive Your truth that sets us free forever. Show us where our Assignment is, because that's the *only place provision is guaranteed for us.* Connect us to the people that can minister to us and bless us financially. They are the chosen channels you are anointing in our life. Bring us back into a place of provision, the place of *obedience.* In Jesus' name. Amen."

You will begin to prosper when you start believing that it is the desire and will of God for you.

❧ 2 ❧

MANY PEOPLE NEVER DREAM BIG ENOUGH TO REQUIRE A FINANCIAL MIRACLE.

Some People Consider Mere Survival A Success.
Five dollars an hour is enough for them. They have no great dreams. Their long-term plans are to attend a movie next week. *They lack vision.* They do not dream of creating an orphanage for 1,000 children; printing one million Bibles for China, or building a television station in a great city. Many people do not even care that their child ever attends college or not. They simply want enough money to go down to Denny's and buy three pancakes and two eggs. That is their idea of a grand slam in the game of life.

Their goal is to get through the day. Most people never taste the surging, powerful and revolutionary Spirit life. They remind me of the singer drawing his last breath in life, "One day at a time, sweet Jesus! That's all I'm asking you for." Sadly, that is the condition of millions today.

Common people set common goals.
Uncommon achievers set uncommon goals.
This cancer of indifference is contagious. It will

destroy every ounce of passion surging through your veins. Maybe this has happened to you. There's nothing big you're trying to do any more with your life. You're not trying to feed the hungry. You're not trying to reach one million people in China with Bibles. You feel nothing when your pastor tells you the vision he sees for the church and your involvement. Nothing is driving you. *Nothing is forcing you away from your present situation.* You have adapted to the common life...while the uncommon achiever within is screaming for attention.

One of the most extraordinary achievers in my generation has been Oral Roberts. I will never forget a statement he once made, "The most dangerous time in your life is when you don't have a need." That's when self sufficiency, like a cancerous growth, begins to form on your life. Smugness seeps into your system. You think God is unnecessary. *Your faith becomes unused.*

Oh my friend, listen to me today! If this is happening to you, run for your life.

> **Get A Future So Big That Today Looks Tiny.**

Get a future so big that today looks tiny. You see, when God gives you a dream, it will be bigger than your present paycheck. *It will require a miracle.*

If your dream doesn't require God, it is not really a God-given dream. *If God gets involved with your dream, He becomes the only means to achieve it.*

You are commanded to *become more.* Increase is expected of you. Read the unforgettable story of the wicked and slothful servant that Jesus discussed in Matthew 25. When he refused to use his talent and gifts, a curse came upon him *because he did not multiply.* "Take therefore the talent from him" (Matthew 25:28). He was punished bitterly. "And cast ye the unprofitable servant into outer darkness: there shall be weeping and gnashing of teeth" (Matthew 25:30).

Listen to the incredible first chapter of the holy ancient writings, "And God blessed them, and God said unto them, Be fruitful, and multiply, and replenish the earth, and subdue it:" (Genesis 1:28).

When I talk to you about a financial Harvest, I am seeing something bigger than going out to eat at a restaurant twice a week. I am talking about the supernatural abundant life...I am talking about living in the *center* of your faith, not the edges.

I had an experience at the Dallas-Fort Worth Airport many years ago. As I spoke to the waitress about her finances, she tossed her hair and said, "I don't like all that preaching about money."

"Wouldn't you like to have more money?" I asked.

"No!" she replied angrily, "that's what's wrong with the world today. Everybody is wanting more and more and more. I have enough for me and my son. That's all I need, and I'm happy!"

I paused. Then, I looked right into her eyes and said, "Have you ever seen any children on television starving to death because of a famine in their country?"

"Yes," she said.

"Have you ever really wished you could help them in a significant way?"

She said impulsively and quickly, "Oh, many times I have wished..." and then her voice trailed off. She stopped. It hit her.

That's what a financial Harvest is all about. Not merely being blessed, but becoming an *instrument of blessing to the hurting around you.*

Financial Harvest is much bigger than simply being able to write out a check for your car payment on time. It's much more powerful than being able to order an extra bag of french fries for your children at McDonald's.

God is looking for Golden Connections on earth. He wants somebody willing to use their faith for supernatural events on this planet.

Get a dream big enough to require the supernatural intervention of God.

Get a dream big enough to require every ounce of faith present in your system.

If you fail to birth the dream God has planted in you like a Seed, you will become angry and bitter. You will lash out at others who are taking giant steps in a small world. You will start talking like a victim instead of a victor.

Faith is confidence in God. It requires an instruction. Faith is activated by needs. When you really do not have a great need in your life, that is a dangerous season. You will be tempted to live life without knowing God. When you fail to reach for God, you become cut off from all the supply, the Source.

"Without faith it is impossible to please Him: for he that cometh to God must believe that He is, and that He is a rewarder of them that diligently seek Him" (Hebrews 11:6).

Always remember this: the day that you say, "I have enough," the extra wave of blessing goes elsewhere to someone who is standing with arms outstretched toward heaven shouting, "I am *expecting* a supernatural wave of blessing."

That's one of the reasons thousands are not receiving a significant and supernatural financial Harvest in their daily life.

Double The Dream You Have Been Nurturing And Your Financial Harvest Will Double!

≈ Psalm 20:7 ≈

"Some trust in chariots, and some in horses:
but we will remember the name of the
Lord our God."

≈ 3 ≈

Some People Believe Their Financial Income Depends On Their Boss Or Loved Ones.

Your Harvest Comes Through People, Not From People.

How do you know when you are depending on men, instead of God? When you get angry at the boss who fails to give you the desired raise. You blame him, not God. When you become furious because a loved one turns you down for a loan, that's the proof that you believe in your heart that your financial source is really them instead of God.

That's why millions will never receive a financial Harvest. *They are sitting at the wrong door waiting for their blessing.*

Yes, it hurts inside when your character, efforts and diligence are not acknowledged by others. But, you must remember *all promotion originates from God:* "For promotion cometh neither from the east, nor from the west, nor from the south. But God is the judge: He putteth down one, and setteth up another" (Psalm 75:6, 7).

You must believe this or you will never experience supernatural increase. *God wants to be trusted.* He will not give His glory to another. He is the Source that put favor in the heart of Potiphar toward Joseph. He is the One who reminded the butler to tell Pharaoh about the gifts of interpretation in Joseph. Joseph went from the prison into the palace within 24 hours. Why? He trusted God, the Source of his promotion. He did not look to men. He depended on God.

David, who also experienced the incredible quickness of a promotion, understood this: "Some trust in chariots, and some in horses: but we will remember the name of the Lord our God" (Psalm 20:7).

Recently, I had the unfortunate experience of sitting at a restaurant table with a circle of complainers. Every one began to explain why their financial circumstances were so dismal.

"My boss is stingy," commented one. "He hasn't given a raise to anybody in our company in over three years." Inside I was shaking my head. It was a never ending conversation. I have heard a thousand similar conversations in my lifetime — people explaining why they have not received their financial Harvest. Fact: they ignored God, their true Source. *You will only nurture a relationship that promises a reward.* If you truly recognize God as your Source, you will continuously be nurturing your relationship with Him. This guarantees your financial future.

It happened for me in Philadelphia. After I walked back to the study, the secretary of the pastor said, "Dr. Mike, we took out one half of your offering tonight for the church."

"Why?"

"Well, we did not know it was going to be this

large of an offering."

I replied, "You received a letter from my office. The policy of our ministry is that the love offering at the conclusion of each service I speak in is given for our ministry outreach and evangelism. It is obvious that you have a problem. Please take the whole entire offering for yourself. I refuse to enter into a controversy over money. I won't touch it. I will not take a penny. I already have a Jehovah-Jireh in my life who will provide for me."

I wasn't trying to be cute or cocky.

If I had thought for one moment that my financial income was dependent on people instead of God, I would have become so angry. But, I remind myself continuously that my true Source is God. He chooses *who* will become the channels to bless my life.

Your own Seed controls your Harvest. It is not the giving of others that determines your income. It is your *own giving* that will determine your income.

I had a powerful experience in one of my Wisdom conferences several years ago. I felt the Holy Spirit speak to me about forty people who would plant a Seed of $10,000. As soon as I spoke, forty people jumped up and came and stood in line, each representing a Seed of $10,000. After we prayed, the Holy Spirit spoke a second instruction to me. "Tell them this is simply an Isaac offering. I just wanted to see if they would be obedient and willing to do as I command. Do not accept their offering. Consider it already given. Tell them to *keep it* and expect 99 more Harvests coming according to My Word in Mark 10:28-30."

Forty people walked back to their seat, and I

was left with "no offering" for my ministry.

Several ministers met in my hotel room after the service. "Mike, how did you feel watching $400,000 walk out of that room?"

Well, I was honest with them. Inside my heart, I had already spent $400,000 on television programs. I was praising God inside, thanking Him for the largest offering I'd ever received in my ministry. But, God had chosen to turn it into a Seed for my future Harvest.

What did this mean? God had just given me the ability to plant a $400,000 Seed in a single day. Had I kept it, that would have been my Harvest. Sowing it made it a Seed, the least it would ever be.

What You Can Walk Away From, You Have Mastered. When you can walk away from money, you have mastered it.

What you walk away from determines what God will bring to you.

Quit looking to men for your financial Harvest.

> **What You Can Walk Away From, You Have Mastered.**

Be thankful. Be gracious when receiving through people. But, keep yourself reminded *every hour of your life* that the Source of every good thing is the One who created you. "But thou shalt remember the Lord thy God: for it is He that giveth thee power to get wealth, that He may establish His covenant which He sware unto thy fathers, as it is this day" (Deuteronomy 8:18).

When you focus your total dependency on God, you will see the most incredible flow of Harvests you have ever experienced in your lifetime.

❦ 4 ❦

Many Do Not Really Respect Money And Do Not Recognize It As A Weapon And Tool For Good.

What You Respect Will Come Toward You.

What You Respect Will Come Toward You.

What you don't respect moves away from you.

Whether it is a miracle or a dog, what you fail to respect will *become uncomfortable in your presence.* Think about a bad restaurant you visited. Remember when they failed to serve you, and you waited forty minutes? When you asked for the ketchup, they looked angry. You were treated as an *interruption* to their day, instead of an answer to their prayers. What did you do? You never went back. Why? *They did not respect you.*

Respect simply means to find someone *important and worthy of protection and pursuit.*

Recently, I did a little opinion poll in several of my meetings.

"How many have been in a financial seminar or consulted a certified financial planner within the last three years?"

It amazed me. Only three out of a hundred had ever sat down with a financial planner.

"Aren't those financial planners pretty expensive," a tall lanky fellow asked after the seminar one night.

"Well, mine cost $200 an hour," I replied. But, don't you agree that $200 is worth spending to find out how to make your $30,000 income multiply?"

Your library reveals the depth of your respect for money. You spent $300 last month on your automobile payment, $130 dollars went to gas, and you spent $800 on your apartment expenses. Now, let's look at your checkbook. Provide me a total of what you invested in books and tapes. Does it compare with your automobile payment? Probably not.

Some believe in their car more than they believe in their future.

Your reluctance to invest money in financial books may reveal little respect for money. For example, if you are 40 years old, you should have in your library at least 40 significant books on wealth, one book a year. That's not too much to ask. Are you 30? Then, you should have 30 significant books on building your financial worth.

Your anger toward ministers who talk about money reveals a lack of true respect.

"Dr. Mike, I think preachers say too much about money," a lady ranted and raved after one seminar. "Why, last Sunday morning, my pastor talked for 15 or 20 minutes about money before the offering. It just killed something inside me. Many of us are so mad, we don't know what to do. It's really hurting our church." How tragic, unfortunate and sad!

This lady probably spent two hours a day sitting in a hot sweaty automobile, in traffic on the freeway... to make money. Then, she worked and toiled 40 hours that week in a smoke infested, foul-mouthed environment... to make money. Then, she complained and cried when her boss failed to give her more money, following her conversation for a raise.

Now, she is infuriated that a man of God would discuss it for 15 minutes. *That's mind damage.*

"But, there are many things more important for a preacher to discuss than money!" some will argue.

Let's look at it a moment. Are you angry with the dentist who refuses to discuss your teeth? Of course not. But, I could easily argue that there's many things on earth that are more important than your broken tooth.

Would you be angry with a lawyer who refused to take your case? Of course. But, I could argue that there are many things much more important than your lawsuit.

Then, why don't you respect a man of God who cares enough about your financial status to help you connect with the master Provider, your Jehovah-Jireh? Unfortunately, secular society has more respect for money than Christianity does. Almost every article in Christian magazines dealing with money is a *warning for pursuing it.* Almost every ministry in America points to the pitfalls of materialism. Meanwhile, someone has said that 40 percent of the bankruptcies involve born-again Christians. Millions cannot even pay their bills. Thousands of dreams are sabotaged and shipwrecked on the rocks of bankruptcy and poverty, while we are worried about the *danger* of money!

Lack of respect is evident when you ridicule and laugh at financial mentors.

"Dr. Mike, I think some preachers are obsessed with money. That's all they talk about. There's one preacher on television that talks about nothing else. He never talks healing, or the coming of Christ, or family problems. His whole focus is money."

Then, answer these simple questions. Are you angry at your dentist because he refuses to cut your hair? Of course not. That's not his focus.

Do you fire your lawyer because he will not mow your grass? Of course not. Legal work is his calling.

You see, every minister is given a different Assignment. Usually, they contain a unique and uncommon anointing (a Divine enablement) for that particular revelation of Wisdom. If you truly *respected* money, you would leap with joy at the discovery of any man of God who could help you move away from poverty into the Land of Plenty.

Lack of respect for money is obvious. *When you make simplistic, sneering and belittling statements such as "Money won't make you happy."* Well, poverty will not make you happy either. There's not even a relationship between the two.

Money is not necessary because it makes you happy.

Money is necessary because it solves problems. "Money answereth all things" (Ecclesiastes 10:19).

If you treat someone wrong, they will move away from you.

When you disrespect someone, they may never enter your door again.

When you disrespect money, your ability to

attract it will vanish.

You must recognize that money is a tool. Your financial Harvest will enable you to help your family, loved ones, and participate in great civic projects such as a hospital, the Red Cross, the March of Dimes or whatever charity is close to your heart. Money is a tool because it enables you to buy the things for your children that educate them, excite them and strengthen their lives.

Money is a weapon against ignorance. Money enables you to go to college, secure a wonderful education, travel around the world, and be a provider instead of a parasite of society.

Money makes you a Burden-Bearer, instead of a burden.

I have often asked those who belittle financial prosperity, "Tell me how many wonderful things that you can do without money. Then, provide me a list of the things that you could accomplish if you had plenty."

They refuse to answer.

Respect money and it will leap toward your life like a deer.

Disrespect money and it will move away from you faster than lightning.

It's one of the main reasons people do not receive their financial Harvest. "For Wisdom is a defence, and money is a defence..." (Ecclesiastes 7:12).

Why is money not respected? Usually, *when it comes too easily to someone,* they do not respect it. You often see this with your children. You give your child a quarter or a dollar. An hour later they don't know what happened to it. They lost it or gave it to someone. Why? It required nothing of them. It became too easy.

You will only protect something in which you have invested.

Asking Is The Proof Of Humility.

Teenagers rarely respect money. At this young age, they have not developed an obsession or passion for a *great goal that requires it.* Their house is provided by daddy. Their food is provided by mother. Their friends give them free transportation. A father, who feels guilty over neglect, shoves a $20 bill in their hand to go to town. If a teenager has not labored and worked hard for their money, they will not develop a respect for it.

You will rarely fight for anything that comes easy.

Money is often not respected *when financial mentors have not been a part of your life.* Everything must be *taught.* Few things are truly instinctive in these areas. If your mother or father experienced the "Depression," they probably emphasize the importance of making "every cent count."

Often, wealthy children are careless with money. Especially if it is handed to them instead of their laboring and working for it.

Recently, I read where one of the wealthiest men in America gives his child only $5.00 a week. He said, "I want him to learn to respect money. If I make it too easy for him, he will not understand how difficult it is to generate."

"I never think about money," was the flippant remark one night by a young man. I looked at him. His clothes were purchased by his father. His car was given to him for a birthday. His college education was paid for by his parents. He was a parasite. He had never done anything significant with his life. It was no wonder to me that he had no respect for money. He had never *earned* any.

When you truly recognize how important the gift of money is, your Harvest will come towards you in miraculous ways.

⇝ Matthew 7:7,8 ⇝

"Ask, and it shall be given you; seek, and ye
shall find; knock, and it shall be opened
unto you: For everyone that asketh
receiveth; and he that seeketh findeth; and
to him that knocketh it shall be opened."

~ 5 ~

SOME PEOPLE NEVER EVEN ASK FOR A SPECIFIC AND SIGNIFICANT FINANCIAL HARVEST.

Asking Is The Key To Receiving.

Jesus made this very clear. "Ask, and it shall be given you; seek, and you shall find; knock, and it shall be opened unto you: For every one that asketh receiveth; and he that seeketh findeth; and to him that knocketh it shall be opened" (Matthew 7:7, 8).

Many *desire* more money.

Many *wish* for more money.

Many *dream* about more money.

But, they never have understood *the power of asking.*

"I really need more money," one elderly lady told me late one night after a lecture.

"How much are you needing?" I asked.

"Oh, I just need more!"

"How much more?"

She was even more persistent. "I just need more, that's all!"

Finally, I pulled a nickel out of my pocket and handed it to her saying, "Your prayers just got answered." You see, she wanted more, and I gave her more.

She was *wanting* more, but she was not really *asking* for more. She never specified an amount.

1. *Many People Rebel Against Asking.* Asking is an irritation to them. You see, asking really is a *portrait of humility.* When you ask somebody for something, you are admitting lack and limitation. That is not valued in our society today.

Self-sufficiency is what our culture treasures.

Asking appears to be a weakness.

Yet, asking *is the Golden Key to receiving.*

2. *Many Refuse To Ask God For A Financial Harvest.* Why? They have disobeyed every instruction He has given them and they know it. This destroys their bravado and boldness.

You can only be bold when you believe you are right.

When you have ignored faithful church attendance, tithing and putting God first, you lack the audacity to approach Him for anything. It's very difficult to spend Sundays on your boat at the lake and then feel comfortable asking God for a financial blessing on Monday morning.

3. *Many Refuse To Ask God For Specific Amounts Of Income.* Why? They do not even know how much they owe their creditors!

Many years ago a young man came to me in desperation. He said, "I'm going bankrupt. I'm going to lose everything I have. Would you help me?"

"Tell me exactly how much you owe your creditors," I replied.

He looked puzzled and bewildered. "I have no idea how much money I owe."

"Well, sit down and make me a list of each

person that you owe, the amount you owe them, and how much you can set aside each month to pay them off completely."

He took the conversation another direction. I brought him back to it. "Stop beating around the bush. Sit down and make me a list of what you actually owe. You cannot use your faith without a target. *Faith requires an instruction.* If faith has an option, it cannot work. It must be given a specific Assignment." (The ancient writings call it double mindedness.) "A double minded man is unstable in all his ways" (James 1:8).

4. *Many Refuse To Ask God In Faith.* They whine, cry and even weep bitterly in church services. But, they refuse to wrap their request with the garments of faith and *expectation.* "Without faith it is impossible to please Him: for he that cometh to God must believe that He is, and that He is a rewarder of them that diligently seek Him" (Hebrews 11:6).

God wants to be believed. His only pain is to be doubted. His only pleasure is to be believed. Every effort of God has one focus — to find a person who believes what He says.

▶ God has an obsession *to be believed.*

▶ He *withholds* from those who doubt, (Isaiah 1:19).

▶ He *rewards* those who believe, (Deuteronomy 28:1-14).

Tears alone do not move God.
Desperation does not intimidate God.
Manipulation does not control God.
Education does not influence God.
Faith is the only voice God respects.

Faith is the only method that impresses God to activate miracles. You *must* ask in faith. *Faith comes when you hear God talk.* "So then faith cometh by hearing, and hearing by the word of God" (Romans 10:17).

5. *Some Do Not Ask Because They Believe That Provision Is Sovereign, Based On The Whim Or Impulses Of God.*

"Mike, if God wants me to have money, He will give it to me," one man said.

So, I replied to this brother, "That means had He wanted you to comb your hair this morning, He would have combed it for you. If He wanted you to wear clothes, you would not have been born naked." How absurd! God wants everyone saved, doesn't He? But many are going to hell. The will of man is involved. Provision is your choice.

6. *Some Do Not Ask God For A Financial Harvest Because They Believe That Money Is A Trap.*

"Don't you think satan gives people a lot of money, so they will go back on God?"

I replied to this lady, "If money can make you backslide, why hasn't satan overdosed you with it?" If money could cause you to move away from God, satan would back a semi-truck to your house and unload $100 bills all over your yard.

7. *Many Never Ask God For Financial Wisdom.* They never enter the Secret Place when they make major purchases such as a house or an automobile. They would never consider fasting three days before accepting a new job or place of employment. They depend on *their own mind and perception.* They *ignore* the Holy Spirit who advises them in all things. In the ancient writings, the early disciples consulted

the Holy Spirit about everything, even the places they would minister. Read these fascinating words, "As they ministered to the Lord, and fasted, the Holy Ghost said, Separate me Barnabus and Saul for the work whereunto I have called them. And when they had fasted and prayed, and laid their hands on them, they sent them away. So they, being sent forth by the Holy Ghost, departed unto Seleucia; and from thence they sailed to Cyprus" (Acts 13:2-4).

They were not moved by the needs of people.

They were moved by *the voice of the Holy Spirit.*

They did not go where they were *needed.*

They ministered where they were *commanded.*

8. *Many Refuse To Ask For A Specific Miracle.*

"I really need a house," said a young man one night.

"Describe the house you're asking God to provide," was my reply.

"Oh, just anything. I just need a house."

You know, God could have given him a dog house and he would not be able to complain. If you are asking God for a specific house, peruse through some magazines until you find a picture of exactly the house you have been asking God to provide. *Focus your faith for it.* If you're asking God for a specific automobile, find the color, the model and the specific car in some magazine and hold that page up to God in intercession daily and believe for your future.

If you are asking Him for a specific financial salary, write the amount on your bulletin board. Inform your circle of intercessors. Hold that sheet of paper high in prayer during your *seasons of intercession* and ask the Lord to show you how to earn that specific salary.

Clarify. Be specific. Focus your faith with precision. Faith will not respond to an uncertain sound. God responds to directness. Persistence. Tenacity.

9. *Few Really Know What They Want Out Of Life Financially.* Precision is rare in conversations. I have sat at restaurant tables while friends have looked into the face of a waitress they have never met in their life and asked, "What do you think I should eat today?" It puzzles me.

I have seen friends purchase clothes that the *salesman* liked! In fact, a salesman that they had never even met before in their lifetime. Think about it! Someone they had never met is making decisions about the clothes they are wearing!

When you ask God for anything:
▶ Ask *specifically.*
▶ Ask *persistently.*
▶ Ask *expectantly.*
▶ Ask *largely.*
▶ Ask *honestly.*

10. *Many Refuse To Ask Their Boss For Anything.* They would rather complain to a fellow employee, whine to their marriage partner, and bellyache to themselves. They refuse to ask their boss for new problems to solve, seminars they should attend, ways they can improve.

They refuse to ask their boss to reconsider their salary and show them a plan for increase.

11. *Many Are Unwilling To Earn What They Want.*

Also, they refuse to ask *at the right time* for any special requests. Several years ago this happened to me. I was weary and tired. I had been flying

2,000 miles. Upon my arrival, my bookkeeper said, "I need to talk to you." She took me into a conference room and proceeded to tell me that she needed $1,000 a month raise, because she and her husband were going to move in a bigger house and wanted more money. Wrong timing played a part.

12. *Many Refuse To Ask The Right People The Right Questions.* Never ask a bankrupt brother-in-law about investments. Never consult the poor for financial wealth. You wouldn't consult a 400 pound man about the quickest way to lose weight, would you?

▶ *Many refuse to ask financial planners to critique their budget and make suggestions.*

▶ *Some refuse to ask creditors for new considerations and debt reductions.*

▶ *Some refuse to negotiate and ask for a lower price on any item.*

You Do Not Have A Right To Anything You Will Not Pursue.

Several years ago, I visited a baggage company here in Dallas.

"I would like a corporate discount," I requested.

"What is a corporate discount?" was the puzzled reply.

"Forty percent off the retail price," I requested.

"All right," was the immediate agreement.

Negotiate everything. EVERYTHING.

You have no right for anything you have not asked for. It would amaze us to see how many things we are not experiencing or possessing... because we refuse to ask.

I have a mental picture of a huge invisible

warehouse. It contains an incredible array of blessings, wall after wall, shelf after shelf. When we arrive in heaven, there may be one huge "Cry Night." It will be a night where tears run like rivers. It will happen after God brings you over to the Warehouse, "I want to show you what you *could* have had, if you would have simply asked Me for it."

"Ye have not, because ye ask not. Ye ask, and receive not, because ye ask amiss, that ye may consume it upon your lusts" (James 4:2, 3).

Remember—God wants you to approach Him when you have a need. He wants to be trusted. He wants to be your Source. He wants to be the Person you discuss every problem with.

Asking is an *acknowledgment of His Wisdom.*

Asking is an *acknowledgment of your humility.*

Asking is one of the most powerful and wonderful Golden Keys to unlocking the Treasure of Supply.

Millions refuse. That's why they have failed to receive everything God wants them to possess, their miracle Harvest.

Ask. Ask appropriately. Ask wisely. Ask humbly. Ask Expectantly...and your Golden Harvest will emerge richer than you ever dreamed.

∞ 6 ∞

Some Do Not Really Believe That They Deserve A Financial Harvest.

Roots Of Inferiority Grow Deep.

I was born and raised in Louisiana. One of the most common explanations of lack and poverty I must have heard a thousand times over the years. "I don't have an education. My father and mama have no education. We're just poor country folks."

I suppose those statements have been spoken into my ears thousands of times, explaining poverty and the lack of financial supply.

You see, thousands are so conscious of their weaknesses and limitations, they cannot even imagine themselves in a beautiful car, luxurious home, and the ability to write out a check for any need. Poverty can become a part of your lifestyle so easily. Many *adapt* to lack.

I'm not talking about a false humility that many put on like a cloak. I am talking about a deep-rooted philosophy or feeling that success is too far away to pursue.

"Well, Mike, I don't deserve anything."

"Then why are you trying to get a place in

heaven?" Do you feel that you deserve that? Do you believe that you have a right to walk on streets of gold, but not have a $50 a month raise? That's absurd. Something is out of balance.

What makes a man dare to ask God for an eternal residence next to the Apostle Paul, but think it is prideful to ask Him for a new car? Now, thankfulness is a beautiful and wonderful quality. Unthankfulness is poisonous. Humility is precious and to be treasured. There's nothing wrong with feeling that God has blessed you beyond what you deserve. Every person who has been in the presence of God for any length of time feels this way. His glory is enough. His forgiveness is enough. It's true, if He never gave us a thing on earth, His presence satisfies every part of our being. It is a wonderful attitude that God treasures.

But, I am focusing on the devastating and poisonous Cancer of Inferiority and loss of confidence that makes a man crawl away from God instead of boldly approaching God.

One lady told me, "I'm afraid money will hurt me spiritually."

"If you feel that financial increase will make you get away from God, why don't you ask the Lord to strip you of one half of your salary, and that will increase your spirituality," I teased.

Late one night after a service, a man approached me feeling, in his words, "unworthy." As he stood, with tears that appeared very real, telling me how unworthy he was of financial blessing, I had several thoughts. I wonder if he tells his boss that, when his boss suggests a raise? Does he lower his price to the bare minimum, when a customer wants to make a purchase? Or, does he negotiate furiously at the table of business? My guess was that he was a master negotiator fighting for every penny he could get his hands on. It was only when the teaching on prosperity focused on his *responsibility* that he was intimidated.

Now, it is true that you must qualify for blessings. Read the 28th chapter of Deuteronomy. The requirement is to obey every law and principle of the Word of God.

Isaiah saw it, "If ye be willing and obedient, ye shall eat the good of the land: But if ye refuse and rebel, ye shall be devoured with the sword: for the mouth of the Lord hath spoken it" (Isaiah 1:19, 20).

Some people do not qualify for the blessing of God. That's why they feel unworthy, unwanted and rejected.

Some refuse financial mentorship. "Poverty and shame shall be to him that refuseth instruction: but he that regardeth reproof shall be honoured" (Proverbs 13:18).

Some are disqualified for a financial Harvest because they refuse to work. "For even when we were with you, this we commanded you, that if any would not work, neither should he eat" (2 Thessalonians 3:10).

Paul saw this. He recommended that every person *withdraw* from those too lazy to produce. "And if any man obey not our word by this epistle, note that man, and have no company with him, that he may be ashamed" (2 Thessalonians 3:14).

Stop your victim vocabulary. Your conversations may be destroying you. When you advertise your wounds, you attract vultures and buzzards. They will circle your life waiting for an opportunity to attack and destroy. "Death and life are in the power of the tongue: and they that love it shall eat the fruit thereof" (Proverbs 18:21).

You may feel unworthy, but do not advertise your weakness and vulnerability. God talked to Jeremiah about discussing his limitations publicly with everyone. "Say not, I am a child: for thou shalt go to all that I shall send thee, and whatsoever I command thee thou shalt speak" (Jeremiah 1:7).

You are commanded to take courage and despise fear. "Be not afraid of their faces: for I am with thee to deliver thee, saith the Lord" (Jeremiah 1:8).

God has not given you the spirit of fear. "For God hath not given us a spirit of fear; but of power, and of love, and of a sound mind" (2 Timothy 1:7).

Your tongue is deciding the currents of your life. "Behold, we put bits in the horses' mouths, that they may obey us; and we turn about their whole body. Behold also the ships, which though they be so great, and are driven of fierce winds, yet are they turned about with a very small helm, whithersoever the governor listeth. Even so the tongue is a little member, and boasteth great things. Behold, how great a matter a little fire kindleth! And the tongue is a fire, a world of iniquity: so is the tongue among our members, that it defileth the whole body, and setteth on fire the course of nature; and it is set on fire of hell. For every kind of beasts, and of birds, and of serpents, and of things in the sea, is tamed, and hath been tamed of mankind: But the tongue can no man tame; it is an unruly evil, full of deadly poison" (James 3:3-8).

When the Holy Spirit controls the words you are

saying, your entire life becomes perfected. "If any man offend not in word, the same is a perfect man, and able also to bridle the whole body" (James 3:2).

Do a brief study on those losers in Scriptures who failed to enter Canaan. It was their unbelief, inferiority and words of doubt that destroyed them. Ten spies had returned full of doubt and unbelief. They had seen grapes, but they feared the giants. "We be not able to go up against the people; for they are stronger than we. And they brought up an evil report of the land which they had searched unto the children of Israel, saying, The land, through which we have gone to search it, is a land that eateth up the inhabitants thereof; and all the people that we saw in it are men of great stature... and we were in our own sight as grasshoppers, and so we were in their sight" (Numbers 13:31-33).

I call this, "the Grasshopper Complex."

Their enemy appeared bigger than their God.

God was focusing on the *grapes of blessing*.

The Israelites focused on the *giants of Canaan*.

They forfeited the promised land of Canaan because of a sense of inability, limitation and unworthiness.

Giants never defeated the Israelites.

Fear within them conquered them.

Why do some people feel unworthy? They listened to somebody else who felt unworthy and incapable. "And all the congregation lifted up their voice, and cried; and the people wept that night" (Numbers 14:1).

▶ Somebody *has* influenced you in your past.

▶ Somebody *is* influencing you today.

▶ Somebody has educated you in weaknesses

and limitations.

▶ Somebody has destroyed the Seeds of faith that could produce any future you desired.

Who are those who have sown *Seeds of slaveship* into your heart? *Who* are those who have made you feel unworthy, inferior and lacking the ability to achieve great things for God?

Somebody who failed to believe the Word of God.

Rise up. You can walk away from Egypt. You can shake off the chains of fear. You don't have to stay where you are. Something bigger is rising up within you today. Something bigger than you've ever known in your whole lifetime.

Tomorrow is simply a moment away. Activate it. Move toward it. Move away from unbelief. Move away from doubters, scorners, and defeated people.

As you move toward faith, mountains will fall at your feet, whimpering for instructions. "For verily I say unto you, That whosoever shall say unto this mountain, Be thou removed, and be thou cast into the sea; and shall not doubt in his heart, but shall believe that those things which he saith shall come to pass; he shall have whatsoever he saith. Therefore I say unto you, What things soever ye desire, when ye pray, believe that ye receive them, and ye shall have them" (Mark 11:23, 24).

Your father may have *abused* you.

Your mother may have *accused* you.

Your boss may have *misused* you.

But, you are still alive and well today. You are a survivor, a success, an overcomer. Look what you've come through, gone over, and raced around.

You are a winner and it's obvious. So, hold your head up high, put your shoulders back and march confidently and boldly toward the remarkable land of grapes, honey and supernatural provision that you have arrived to. They were made for *somebody*. Why not *you*?

▶ You were born to taste the grapes.
▶ You are a Giant Killer.
▶ You are a Mountain-Mover.
▶ You can walk through fire and *not be burned.*
▶ The waters of life have *not* overflowed you.

You are worthy to receive what you need because you are the offspring, the child of the Most High God who made the heavens and the earth. "A thousand shall fall at thy side, and ten thousand at thy right hand; but it shall not come nigh thee" (Psalm 91:7).

You can overcome any sickness and disease. "There shall no evil befall thee, neither shall any plague come nigh thy dwelling" (Psalm 91:10).

You are surrounded by angels that guard over you carefully. "For He shall give His angels charge over thee, to keep thee in all thy ways. They shall bear thee up in their hands, lest thou dash thy foot against a stone" (Psalm 91:11, 12).

You are afraid of nothing. "Thou shalt not be afraid for the terror by night; nor for the arrow that flieth by day;" (Psalm 91:5).

You will not die early but live to glorify God. "With long life will I satisfy him, and show him My salvation" (Psalm 91:16).

You will never be without access to God. "Whither shall I go from Thy spirit? or whither shall I flee from Thy presence? If I ascend up into heaven, Thou art there: if I make my bed in hell, behold, Thou art there" (Psalm 139:7, 8).

You will constantly and continuously be led by the Mentor of your life, the Holy Spirit. "If I take the wings of the morning, and dwell in the uttermost parts of the sea; Even there shall Thy hand lead me, Thy right hand shall hold me" (Psalm 139:9, 10).

You are a rare, meticulously sculptured jewel in the crown of God. "For I am fearfully and wonderfully made: marvellous are Thy works; and that my soul knoweth right well" (Psalm 139:14).

God is continuously thinking wonderful and exciting thoughts toward you. "How precious also are Thy thoughts unto me, O God! how great is the sum of them! If I should count them, they are more in number than the sand: when I awake, I am still with thee" (Psalm 139:17, 18).

You will be revived in the midst of any trouble. "Though I walk in the midst of trouble, Thou wilt revive me" (Psalm 138:7).

Your enemies will become the enemies of God. "Thou shalt stretch forth Thine hand against the wrath of mine enemies, and Thy right hand shall save me" (Psalm 138:7).

You will see every miracle completed that God started in your life. "The Lord will perfect that which concerneth me" (Psalm 138:8).

Sin makes you feel unworthy. So, repent. Turn away. "That if thou shalt confess with thy mouth the Lord Jesus, and shalt believe in thine heart that God hath raised Him from the dead, thou shalt be saved" (Romans 10:9).

Memories of disappointments can weaken you and remove your confidence. So, follow the instruction of the Prophet Isaiah. "Remember ye not the former things, neither consider the things of old.

Behold, I will do a new thing; now it shall spring forth; shall ye not know it? I will even make a way in the wilderness, and rivers in the desert" (Isaiah 43:18, 19).

Remember, it is the greatness of God that brings blessing, not our personal greatness. It is your need that attracts His intervention. "For I will pour water upon him that is thirsty, and floods upon the dry ground: I will pour My spirit upon thy Seed, and My blessing upon thine offspring" (Isaiah 44:3).

Some are not experiencing financial Harvest because they are focusing on themselves, their unworthiness and inabilities.

So, change your focus today. Stop analyzing your unworthiness. Focus again on the Author and the Finisher, the Alpha and the Omega, the Beginning and the End of your faith. *He alone is worthy of your total focus.* He is worthy of your attention. He is the Source of every good thing. "Not that we are sufficient of ourselves to think anything as of ourselves; but our sufficiency is of God;" (2 Corinthians 3:5).

Many do not feel they are worthy or deserving of any good thing. That's why their faith has not brought them into His presence to receive the miracle Harvest they deserve.

Come boldly to His throne today. May we pray a brief prayer? "Father, You respond to boldness. Needs do not move You. Desperation does not change You. *Faith* influences You. So, today, thank You for receiving us as we boldly approach Your throne in our time of need. We do not come to You based on our own worthiness and abilities because our righteousness is as filthy rags. Man in his best state is vanity. You respond to hunger, so we reach for You today. You will not disappoint us. In the name of Jesus. Amen."

≈ 7 ≈

MANY RELY UPON THEIR OWN ABILITIES INSTEAD OF THE SUPERNATURAL POWER OF GOD.

The Spirit Of Self-Sufficiency Is A Deadly Trap.
Millions do not pursue the principles of God or invest any time alone with Him in the Secret Place. They are confident, cocky and arrogant. They "need nobody." *The principle is, "If it is to be, it is up to me."*

Now, at first glance, this looks like a wonderful philosophy. It shows willingness to take responsibility. It reveals boldness and strength.

But, God will not let you succeed alone.
In His system, you will fail without a total dependency upon Him. He will see to it.

God rewards humility. "And Samuel said, When thou wast little in thy own sight, wast thou not made the head of the tribes of Israel, and the Lord anointed thee king over Israel?" (1 Samuel 15:17).

The Prophet Samuel showed King Saul how he had deteriorated from the attitude of humility exhibited at his beginning of kingship. The old nature of Adam is still within us. It craves self-sufficiency, a separation from God. It may appear wonderful and humble that you do not need nor pursue the participation of God in your financial Harvest, but it is folly, stupid, and tragic.

It will take more than hard work for an Uncommon Harvest.

It will require more than overtime on your job.

It will require more than extra seminars and books.

An Uncommon Harvest Requires An Uncommon Provider.

An Uncommon Harvest Requires An Uncommon Provider. God knows this. *He will not stop creating crises until you discover it.* "It is good for me that I have been afflicted; that I might learn Thy statutes" (Psalm 119:71).

Your hard work and efforts are wonderful *Seeds*.

Your willingness to sit under college mentorship and invest hours in research is so commendable. It is recognized and *always rewarded*.

But, never be so foolish as to pursue a Harvest that doesn't require the supernatural intervention of an Uncommon Provider, your Jehovah-Jireh. Nothing you could ever produce for yourself will satisfy the *eternity* part of you.

The invisible you requires an invisible God.

The impure part of you requires a pure God.

The untaught part of you requires a Mentor and Teacher, the Holy Spirit.

Millions forfeit a financial Harvest because they see *themselves* as their own source of every blessing.

The pride of Nebuchadnezzar almost destroyed him. He too became self-reliant and said about himself, "Is not this great Babylon, that I have built for the house of the kingdom by the might of my power, and for the honour of my majesty?" (Daniel 4:30).

God responded quickly. "The same hour was the thing fulfilled upon Nebuchadnezzar: and he was driven from men, and did eat grass as oxen, and his body was wet with the dew of heaven, till his hairs were grown like eagle's feathers, and his nails like bird's claws" (Daniel 4:33).

It is a dangerous and tragic thing to become your own god. You are not the only person involved in the miracle cycle of a financial Harvest. *God is your true Source.*

Self-Sufficiency Infuriates God. He will never let you forget it.

Self-Sufficiency Infuriates God.

"Because thou sayest, I am rich, and increased with goods, and have need of nothing; and knowest not that thou art wretched, and miserable, and poor, and blind, and naked: I counsel thee to buy of Me gold tried in the fire, that thou mayest be rich; and white raiment, that thou mayest be clothed, and that the shame of thy nakedness do not appear; and anoint thine eyes with eyesalve, that thou mayest see. As many as I love, I rebuke and chasten: be zealous therefore, and repent" (Revelation 3:17-19).

God monitors every conversation that reveals self-worship. "This will I do: I will pull down my barns, and build greater; and there will I bestow all my fruits and my goods... But God said unto him, Thou fool, this night thy soul shall be required of thee:" (Luke 12:18-20). Jesus warned, "So is he that layeth up treasure for himself, and is not rich toward

God" (Luke 12:21).

When I see unbelievers ignore church yet pull their boat down the freeway toward the beach on Sunday, I see someone who has made himself his god. He ignores the house of God, his pastor, and thinks that it is permissible to neglect the assembling of himself with other believers. He really believes that God has nothing to do with his financial Harvest. He is confident of his abilities, his ability to make progress in a busy world. He doesn't realize he is one heartbeat away from his deathbed every moment.

His prayerlessness is proof of his ignorance (Proverbs 3:5, 6). He trusts his own abilities.

He has excluded God.

This is one of the reasons millions never receive their financial Harvest. "When thou hast eaten and art full, then thou shalt bless the Lord thy God for the good land which He hath given thee. Beware that thou forget not the Lord thy God, in not keeping His commandments, and His judgments, and His statutes, which I command thee this day: Lest when thou hast eaten and art full, and hast built goodly houses, and to dwelt therein; And when thy herds and thy flocks multiply, and thy silver and thy gold is multiplied, and all that thou hast is multiplied; Then thine heart be lifted up, and thou forget the Lord thy God, which brought thee forth out of the land of Egypt, from the house of bondage" (Deuteronomy 8:10-14).

Recognize the importance of God. Become addicted to His presence, dependent upon His counsel and you will discover financial success like *you never imagined.*

≈ 8 ≈

MANY NEVER FULLY GRASP THE IMPACT, INFLUENCE AND MIRACLES THAT AN UNCOMMON HARVEST COULD PRODUCE FOR OTHERS.

Look at the young pianist practicing at the piano. He has a small gift. It is a Seed. It will become his Harvest. He becomes renown around the world as millions buy his albums. He is worth millions because of the impact of his music. *Something he had in his present became much bigger in his future.*

Something You Have In Your Present Can Become Much Bigger In Your Future.

Think about the brilliant mind of Albert Einstein. He had a *Seed of curiosity*. It became the Bridge to brilliance. He understood some scientific principles like no human who had ever lived before him. *Something in his present became much bigger in his future.*

David walks into an army camp with a slingshot

in his back pocket. It was something in his present that became much bigger in his future. *It brought him into the kingship of Israel* as thousands of women danced in the streets honoring him after the death of Goliath.

A small boy hands five loaves and two fishes into the hands of Jesus. *It was his Seed.* It contained something much bigger *when the hands of Jesus touched it.*

Most people never grasp this. *What you presently possess that looks tiny, small and insignificant is incredibly huge, powerful and overwhelming when it arrives in your future.*

Most never even grasp the power of their Seed! So, how can they understand the power of their *Harvest?*

I was in Kansas City. I shared the testimony about my Seed of $58 and the results that had occurred in many lives because of it. After my message, a little boy walked up to me. I had no idea what his name was or anything. The Spirit nudged my heart. "Give him a $100 bill." I was a little shocked. "He's too little. I could give him a dollar and he would not know the difference," I responded. The Holy Spirit insisted. So I reached inside my pocket, rather reluctantly, and handed him the $100 bill. A few minutes later, a little girl walks up. It turns out that she is his sister. The Holy Spirit said, "Give her a $100 bill also." I did not know her name, and still do not know her name. But, I understood the voice of the Holy Spirit. I handed her a $100 bill from my wallet.

Then a woman walked up. It turned out that she was their mother. She was shocked when she saw her two children holding $100 bills in their hands. She blurted out, "What is this for?"

"The Holy Spirit just told me to give it to them," I explained.

She began to cry. She explained, "Tonight you told every one of us to plant a Seed of $58 to represent the 58 kinds of blessings of the Bible. When I went through my purse with tears in my eyes, I was so disheartened. You see, my husband left me three weeks ago. He has refused to help us financially at all. When the children and I came to church tonight, we did not have a can of food in our pantry. No milk in the refrigerator. No food at all. We are broke. When I emptied my purse during the offering, I looked for every penny I could find, every nickel, to find the $58 dollars. I did not have it. But, the total amount of money that I found in my purse was 58 cents. So, I said, Lord, I am planting this 58 cents as a memorial that I want you to remember me. I have confidence you're going to bless me with all 58 blessings." She kept crying. She said, "Now, my children and I can go to an all-night grocery store and buy $200 worth of groceries for our family." I can't tell you how much that blessed and lifted my heart.

You see, my $200 was my Harvest God had provided for *me*. I had no idea that I could create a forever memory in a small family who lacked food and desperately needed a demonstration of God for their life. You cannot believe how powerful your Harvest can be *until you concentrate on the good it can do.*

Someone complained, "I don't believe in all this prosperity teaching." How sad! Are you shrinking your goals to accommodate your financial lack? Are you willing to forfeit your dreams to accommodate your small Harvest?

Or, are you determined to be used by God to make your Harvest an incredible *tool for good?*

Not everybody is pursuing their Harvest so they can stay at the shopping center a little longer. Millions of Christians ache to help a minister in India, build a family life center for their pastor, walk through a Christian bookstore and buy $500 worth of books for their children's library.

Yes, it is true. Thousands sneer, ridicule and scorn ministers of the gospel attempting to unlock their flow of faith for a financial turnaround. They sneer, "Money, money, money. That's all he talks about is more money." They have missed the point. Satan dreads your Harvest. He knows it's future. *Do you?* Can you grasp the amount of incredible things you can make happen for others... *after your Harvest arrives?*

Many never think beyond the moment of their Seed sowing.

They cannot imagine or grasp the unbelievable impact they could make *for good... after their Harvest* arrives. So, they never plant big Seed. They never make big plans. They never use great faith.

They cannot fully grasp the potential impact their one hundredfold Harvest will have on the earth, *so they never reach.*

It explains one of the major reasons people never receive a financial Harvest.

Her name was Sister Maxwell. She was an old lady attending my father's church. Every few weeks she would shove a $5.00 bill and a $10.00 bill in my mother's hand saying, "I want to help send little Michael Dean to Bible school." I was 17 years old. My family had no money to send me. I didn't have enough money to buy a plane ticket to go. But, she took her supply, her personal financial Harvest, and began to sow into my life to send me to Bible school.

I went.

While attending, an old missionary preached a sermon one day at chapel that changed my life forever. He called the message, "Burn your plow." He instructed us students to do like Elisha did and burn the plow of self-sufficiency and give our lives to follow our ministries. I laid on the floor of the auditorium for the entire day. I skipped classes. I cried like a baby. I made up my mind that God could have *every part of me unreservedly.* I was willing to give up anything to preach this gospel for Him the rest of my life.

That was 12,000 services ago, 31 years ago, and 36 countries ago.

Thousands have accepted Christ. Several thousand have accepted the call into the ministry. I could not begin to count the many miracles that have occurred... because a little woman named Sister Maxwell took part of *her* Harvest and helped inspire me to go into Bible school.

Her Harvest was my bridge into my ministry.

It is possible that I might not have gone to Bible school, nor heard that sermon, had she not used part of her Harvest as an exit from my present into my future.

Every dollar in your hand can become a door for someone in prison somewhere.

Somebody will be delivered because of *your Harvest.*

Grasp that. See it. Shout over it and get happy.

When you really realize the incredible Potential Impact you can make when your financial Harvest arrives, your FAITH will leap. That faith is the magnet that attracts the Supernatural Financial Harvest you long to experience.

❧ 9 ❧

Many Do Not Recognize The Seed Or The Soil When They See It.

————◦►●◄◦————

A Seed is a tiny beginning with a huge future.

A Seed Is Anything That Blesses Somebody.

It is anything that can *become* more. It is the *Beginning*. It is anything you can *do, know* or *possess* that can improve the life of another.

Your *Thoughts* are Seeds for desired behavior, conduct and creativity.

Your *Love* is a Seed for relationships.

Your *Time* is a Seed.

Your *Patience* is a Seed.

Your *Money* is a Seed.

Your *Kindness* is a Seed to others.

Your *Prayers* are Seeds.

Stopping slander is a Seed.

Thankfulness is a Seed.

Your Seed is anything you have received from God that can be traded for something else.

You are a walking warehouse of Seeds. Most people do not even know this. They have no idea how many Seeds they contain that can be planted into the lives of others.

▶ Anything that improves another is a *Seed*.

▶ Anything that makes another smile is a *Seed*.

▶ Anything that makes someone's life easier *is a Seed*.

Millions are so busy studying what they do not have they usually overlook something they have already received.

Certainly you must inventory your own needs. But it is more important to inventory your Seeds. Stop focusing on what you *do not* have, and look closer at something you *already have been given*.

Moses did. He complained that he could not talk. God instructed him to shut up and acknowledge the rod in his hand. That was his Seed. His tool to create his future.

David complained that he could not use the armor of Saul. God instructed him to look back at the slingshot he possessed. God always gives you something that can *begin* your future.

Something You Have Been Given Will Create Anything Else You Have Been Promised.

Something You Have Been Given Will Create Anything Else You Have Been Promised.

Little things birth big things. Acorns become oak trees.

One of my associate evangelists has some remarkable qualities that will make him succeed with his life. He is willing to be corrected. He never pouts, never sulks, never withdraws. When he makes a mistake, he is swift to admit it. He does not have a lazy bone in him.

His golden attitude is a golden Seed.

So, when God provided some extra finances for my ministry, the first thing I wanted to do is purchase him a suit. Why? His Seeds of kindness, faithfulness and love *were working.* His Harvest was inevitable.

Most people have no idea what a Seed really is.

Showing up at work *on time...* is a Seed.

Showing up *ahead of time* is another Seed. You see, anything that you can do to make life easier for your boss or anyone else... is a Seed.

Millions have never used ten percent of the Seed stored within them. You see, mowing the grass for your church is a Seed. Baby-sitting for a struggling single parent is a Seed.

You are a living collection of Seeds, a warehouse of powerful, tiny golden passionate *beginnings.*

You must recognize the Seeds God has already stored within you. Your Seed is any gift, skill, or talent that God has provided for you to sow into the lives of others around you. Don't hide it. Use your Seed. Celebrate the existence of Seeds in your life... that are carving the road to your future. Even Joseph recognized his ability to interpret dreams. He wanted to help others. When Pharaoh became troubled, Joseph had a Seed to sow toward his life. "A man's gift maketh room for him, and bringeth him before great men" (Proverbs 18:16).

One of the greatest stories in ancient writings is in 1 Kings 17. Elijah was being fed by ravens at the brook, Cherith. When the brook dried up and the raven failed to show, God gave him a new instruction to go to Zarephath, a small village in Zidon. There, a widow would receive an instruction to provide food for him. When he arrived at the widow's, the scene was dismal and tragic. She was out gathering two sticks (I'll call them two pancakes). Her son lay emaciated on his deathbed in her little house.

Yet, the man of God spoke boldly to her to plant a Seed and give him some of her food.

Her supply had run out. She had no faith for survival. She had no faith for provision. She was looking at her last meal on earth for her and her son.

Now, imagine the instructions from the man of God. "Take one of those pancakes and give it to me." She could have easily said, "Every one of you preachers have been trying to get my pancakes. I received ten letters this week from television preachers wanting to share this pancake."

But, Elijah starts giving instructions that are Scriptural. *His instructions were Seeds.* He was sowing them toward the widow. "Would you get some water for me? While you're at it, would you bring me a little meal?"

"I can't do that. I don't have enough for all of us. Just enough for me and my son."

Elijah explained patiently, "I understand that. You're wise to take care of your son. I want you to do that. But, *first* bring something to me as a man of God. Sow it as a beginning, *a Seed.*"

Then, he suddenly gives her a *reason for sowing.* No, he does not pull out his newsletter and show her a photograph of a dead bird who never showed back up to feed him. He made no reference to the brook drying up. He never told her that his ministry was over and he would starve if she did not cook him a meal.

Rather He showed her a picture of a future. Something that she had not noticed. He revealed to her that something she already had in her possession *was the golden key to getting into her future.* He gave her a picture of the potential supply, the Harvest. (1 Kings 17:14)

You need somebody to help you sow the Seed you already possess. You need someone to show you a picture of the future within it.

> **Something You Already Possess Is Your Key To Your Future.**

Develop an appreciation for the man of God who helps you *discover your Seed,* and provides a photograph of the Harvest *you can expect.*

Elijah did it. It turned a poor woman into a miracle woman. From poverty to plenty. From famine to supply.

You see, most people have not even noticed something *they already have* that can create their future.

Your time is a Seed.

It will produce what money cannot. A friend of mine was brokenhearted. His teenage son had received a car, world travel tickets, and still hated his father.

"Change the Seed if you do not like the Harvest you are producing," I said. "Stop the money flow. Provide him two hours a day for 14 days of nonjudgmental time. *Give him what he cannot find anywhere else and he will return to you.* Create a non-critical climate. Permit him to talk and discuss anything with you for two hours a day. Document what occurs." Two weeks later they became best buddies, going fishing in the morning. The crisis was over. *He found a Seed that would produce the desired result.*

Time is a precious thing. *Wherever* you sow it, something incredible will *grow.*

Think of the huge space called eternity. God reached into it and took a chunk of it and placed it on earth, calling it *Time.* Imagine Him saying, "Here is Time. You can trade it for anything else you want on earth." He did not give you friends. He gave you Time. You sowed Time into others and created strong friendships. God has never "handed" you any money. He gave you Time. You went to someone with money and exchanged your Time for their money. Your boss has money, and you have *"Time"* in the way of work to trade with.

Time is the currency on earth.

France has the franc. Germany has the marc. Japan has the yen. England has the pound. Mexico has the peso. America has the dollar.

Your currency on earth is Time. God gave you Time to exchange for *anything else that was important to you.*

I have never met a poor person who was really conscious of the importance of *Time.* I have never met a wealthy person who was *not* aware of the importance of Time. You see, your Time is a precious gift from God.

Time is your Seed that can produce what money cannot buy.

Imagine this scenario with me for a moment. You happen to be in the office when your boss leans back in his chair and sighs, "I sure wish I had a good glass of carrot juice." Let me show you a few responses that usually occur:

1. $5.00 an hour employee: "I'd like to have a glass of carrot juice too!"
2. $6.00 an hour employee: "You like carrot juice! I like cokes myself."
3. $7.00 an hour employee: "If I had some carrots, I'd make you some."
4. $8.00 an hour employee: "Would you like for me to find someone to make you some?"
5. Employee who can decide his own salary: "I will be right back, sir, within 20 minutes." He returns with a glass of carrot juice requesting more information. "Would you like this daily at a specific time? It can happen, sir."

That is Seed sowing.

Every time your boss is disappointed, you have a chance to prove your uniqueness and significance. Every time you see him unhappy, it is a potential to a promotion. Look, look and *look again* for opportunities to plant a Seed. They surround you every day. *Hundreds of them.*

The Soil Is Any Person You Are Capable Of Helping.

Every Seed is a Golden Door from your present into your future.

If you do not recognize a Seed, how could you ever recognize the Harvest from it?

If a farmer has never seen what a kernel of corn looks like, do you think he would recognize a field of stalks of corn on the side of the road? Of course not. You cannot begin to recognize a Harvest until you recognize a Seed — something precious within you God has enabled you to *know, do* or *possess* and sow.

You are a Walking Warehouse of Seeds. Invest

Time in the Secret Place — your personal place of prayer. Ask the Holy Spirit to show you what you have been given, supernaturally and naturally to plant into the lives of others. Your future is in your own hands.

▶ You can *see something* nobody else can see.

▶ You already *know something* others do not know.

▶ You *can solve problems* others cannot solve. Solving them is your Seed that brings any kind of Harvest you desire.

Millions have no idea what a Seed really is, so they never receive the Harvest from it because it goes unplanted and unsown.

Discover the Seeds you have already received from God and your future can be anything you desire.

∞ 10 ∞

Many People Do Not Recognize A Harvest When It Does Arrive.

Harvests Occur Daily In Your Life.

What is a Harvest? A Harvest is *any good thing God sends into your life.*

It is *any person* who blesses, encourages, corrects, strengthens or improves you.

It is *any idea* planted by your Creator that has potential for helping others.

It is *any opportunity* to increase your finances, maximize your standard of excellence or unlock a gift or skill within you. It is any opportunity you have to solve a problem.

Almost nobody recognizes a Harvest when it occurs.

My mother was a Harvest to me. I cannot believe she raised seven of us children and still kept her joy. She insisted on two family altars every day, two times a day. Every morning and every night. She forced us to memorize a Scripture every day of our life. She insisted I attend youth camps and sit and hear the Word of God daily. She refused to permit me to attend any "ungodly events."

She was the one who continuously spoke into my ears always saying, "Son, always remember to whom much is given, much is going to be required." She was the one who listened when the battles were raging. She was the one who told me when I was wrong.

She was a *major* and wonderful Harvest in my life. Did I recognize that as a teenage boy? Not at all. I hated doing dishes. I thought that mothers had children so they could have "free servants" doing all the work at the house. I really believed that! (If you will listen to teenagers around the kitchen table after a meal, you'll rarely find one who has recognized their parents as Harvests from God!)

My father is a powerful Golden Harvest in my life. He has prayed six to ten hours every day that I can recall. He is 83 years old today, still full of Jesus. He is obsessed with Scripture. I have never heard him tell a lie, curse, or say one sentence that could not be placed on the front page of a newspaper anywhere. He walks with God. My greatest and most familiar memory is him on his knees with his hands uplifted and praying in a heavenly language.

He was a strong disciplinarian. His whippings last in my memory in an unforgettable way. I never heard him raise his voice once in my lifetime. He never screamed. Mother never yelled at any of us. I am still saying, "Yes sir." And, "No sir." You see, he is a gift from God because he *warned, disciplined, and kept me in the presence of God.*

Your Harvests Are Coming Toward You Every Moment.

> *Your Harvests Are Coming Toward You Every Moment.*

I had spoken for a major trucking company several times. Every Christmas, it has been my privilege to speak there. My last visit to Ohio, a trucker came up, "Mike, you told us about planting that Seed of $58 the last time you were here. But, nothing happened. It didn't work for me."

"You didn't get any Harvest at all?" I asked.

"Nope. Nothing."

He kept some small talk going while my mind raced for an appropriate question. You see, I think any man who could look God in the face and say that he has never received anything from the hand of God has a serious problem. (Wisdom may not *always* make you bold, but I am certain ignorance always makes you bold.) We talked awhile. In a few minutes, he stated, "You know, something crazy happened a few weeks ago. I was driving down this freeway over here, and my semi and my trailer jack-knifed. Practically came off the freeway. Could have killed me. Luckily, I got out without a scratch. Crazy, isn't it?"

This is the same man who told me five minutes before, "It didn't work for me. I've never received a Harvest from my Seed."

I'll tell you again. *Almost nobody recognizes a Harvest when it occurs.* He could have been paralyzed from his neck down. A leg could have been chopped off. He could have died leaving his family without a provider. His *safety* was a Miracle Harvest, but he never recognized it.

Every night you are permitted the privilege of driving into your garage, look up at that beautiful moon and stop and say, *"Thank you for another beautiful* Harvest today, Father."

You see, He kept His angels around you every moment of the day. You did not wake up in a hospital with tubes running from your body. Sir, listen to me. *That's a Harvest.*

Thousands never made it back home today, *but you did.*

When you wake up in the morning breathing, alive and well, look out your window. *If you can see a sun rising in the morning,* beautiful and glowing, you've just received *another* Harvest. Thousands have never seen a sunrise *in their lifetime.*

When you sit down tonight at supper, look carefully at the bowls full of food. You can eat until you're stuffed and overflowing. *That's a Harvest.* I can take you to parts of the world such as Calcutta, India, where children die every single night because they could not find enough crumbs in the trash to survive another day.

When you swallow your food and digest it, you've just received *another Harvest.* Thousands are in hospitals this very moment who cannot feed themselves.

When you drove in the traffic this morning, en route to a full day's work, you just received *another Harvest.* Millions would give anything today if they knew their *reason* to wake up. But, they're unemployed. They're looking for a place of significance.

You've just received *another Harvest.*

Can you hear the incredible music coming across the wind, or from your stereo? Thousands cannot hear a sound. But you've just received *another Harvest.* As you lay your head on your pillow tonight, stare at the ceiling a few moments. It may rain, but you will not be disturbed. The winds may blow hard, but you will not sense it. Lightning may flash, but you are safe. You have a shelter over your head. You're cozy.

God has just given you *another Harvest*.

When your child comes running up to you saying, "Daddy, Daddy," you throw your arms out and welcome that child. You see, thousands of parents have lost their children. Disease, accidents, irreversible situations have created a great vacuum within them. Their house is silent, screaming with the loneliness. That mother would give anything in the world to hear her child cry in the middle of the night. The father would trade every penny in his savings account to see his little boy run across the yard just one more time. Your children are around you today.

You have just received *another Harvest* from the Father who loves you.

As I awakened this morning, I swung my legs to the side of the bed. I sat there, then moved into the bathroom where I punched "play" on my cassette player. I began to hear the deep, powerful rich voice speaking the Scriptures aloud on the cassette. My heart begins to throb. Something in me begins to feel the energy of the supernatural God I serve.

You see, I have just received *another Harvest*.

I have found the incredible healing oil, the Word of God, that heals the wounds of my life. Yet, millions are unsaved, unchanged, and untaught. I have *learned*. I have *discovered*. I have *Jesus*. He has changed my life.

I have received *another Harvest*.

As you sit in your beautiful car today, air

conditioned and safe, replay in your mind the thousands of refuges who are crawling across the desert tonight looking for a tent where they can take their family and drink a cup of water. A slice of bread is celebrated by them. They have lost their home due to the war and conflicts in their country. You will see it on the news every night of your life. Yet, you will pull up at a restaurant in a few hours, purchase a hamburger, and complain because something has been left off the sandwich. Perhaps the pickles or you received mustard instead of mayonnaise. But, you will find something to complain about. By the way, don't forget your Harvests. Oh, my friend, unthankfulness was the first sin, and God has not forgotten.

Your life has been a parade of Harvests.

See, you must learn to *recognize* your Harvest. Your Harvest is *any person or anything that can bless or benefit you.* It may be someone who can contribute something you need — information, favor, finances, an explosive idea or encouragement when you need it most. A Harvest is when somebody recommends you to another person. This creates the flow of favor and acceptance toward your life. *Access to someone who believes you is a Harvest.*

Your Harvest already exists.

It is walking around you! Just as your eyes had to be opened to recognize Jesus, your eyes also must be opened to *recognize your Harvests* as they come. The entire world missed the *Harvest of Jesus.* "He was in the world, and the world was made by Him, and the world knew Him not. He came unto His own, and His own received Him not" (John 1:10, 11). How tragic! Spiritual leaders, such as the Pharisees, failed to recognize Him! Politicians of His day *failed to see Him as their Harvest.*

That's why I am baffled, bewildered and angered at the vicious, malicious, unexplainable attack on the message of sowing Seed for a Harvest. Recently, I wept before a large group of ministers and cried out, "Will somebody explain to me why Offering Time is so painful for you? Please tell me why you can spend two hours on Friday night sponsoring a basketball game for your teenagers, but you think fifteen minutes in a service discussing the Seed and the Harvest is *too long?* Please explain that! Somebody tell me why it's permissible to sit for 90 minutes at a 24 hour restaurant for pancakes after church, but a 90 minute message on prosperity from the hand of the Multiplier and Provider aggravates, agitates and infuriates us?   Please explain to me. Tell me why an offering turns you off!"

"Somebody please tell me why it was all right for Jesus to die like a dog on Calvary; eight inches of thorns crushed into His brow; a spear in His side and spikes in His hands; 400 soldiers spitting on His body; 39 stripes tearing His back to shreds; His beard ripped off His face. Yet talking about bringing a dime out of each dollar back to the House of God infuriates those who claim to be obsessed with Him and His will. Will somebody please explain that?"

What do you have that God did not give you?

It is He that keeps breathing His breath into you. You could not breath another minute if God did not breath into you.

You could not walk another step *if God were not there.*

You couldn't live another day *if His presence*

were withheld from you.

Everything you possess *came from Him.*

Everything you will ever own in your future *must come from Him.*

I looked at hundreds of pastors in Washington, DC, and cried out, "Please explain why you are embarrassed to celebrate sowing a Seed into the work of Jesus Christ! *Why? Why? Why?* Why is that so humiliating to you? Why are you so bold and audacious and brash enough to ask God for a continuous *stream of miracles* for everybody in your church, yet you don't have enough boldness to look in the face of your people and instruct them to bring an offering to the front and place it openly and joyfully in His hand? Why? Is it a reward for a boxer to receive $14 million dollars for 90 seconds of boxing? Another athlete receives $40 million for bouncing a basketball. Yet, why is bringing 10 cents to God so burdensome to us.

Why is it painful for us to ask somebody for $20 to spread the name of Jesus, the greatest name on earth that brings men out of hell into heaven?

Oh, listen to me. Hear my heart today. When your pastor receives an offering, he has just *opened the door for you to change the seasons of your life.* You can whine about it. Complain about it. Sneer and ridicule. You may even say idiotic things like, "I am so glad our pastor never talks about money." Frankly, I would never attend a church that didn't discuss money often. You see, I think about supply every day of my life. The last thing I need is someone who ignores the greatest needs in my life!

Some board members recently discussed the salary of their pastor with me. They were concerned.

They felt his income might be a little larger than necessary.

"Is your family ready for heaven should they die?" I asked. "Whose teaching has sustained them and kept them close to God?"

As we talked, their eyes widened. They understood. They were actually considering lowering his salary, yet he was the man who was the *Prayer Covering* over their lives, *driving back the darkness of error, smashing the locks* on their mental prisons, and *bringing them into the presence of God* whose peace and joy was multiplied in their lives. Their pastor had changed them forever. But they did not recognize him as their Harvest.

It is possible that your miracle Harvest is going past you every day.

You are failing to see it. Failing to appropriate it. Failing to be *thankful* for it.

You must stop what you are doing long enough to see what is happening around you.

You are moving toward something wonderful. Something marvelous is also moving toward you. Can you slow down long enough to discern it?

Nobody else can do it for you. Nobody.

Nobody else *should* do it for you.

You are responsible for your life, your Seed, and your Harvests.

"Oh, I wish I could try one more time," a woman cried. "I made a huge mistake with my husband. It was my fault. He was the greatest man I ever knew, but I managed to find flaws and things I did not like about him. I want to go back home, but I can't."

It was too late. *Her Harvest had gone through her fingers.* It was over.

Often I hear, "Dr. Mike, I give and give and give, but God never gives it back to me. I never receive the Harvest. What should I do?"

That question haunts me. How could any person who had any discerning at all of the blessings of God stand boldly and unashamedly and say, "God never blesses me?" It's explainable. That individual has no idea what a Harvest even looks like.

Do you?

Oh, friend, recognize any ingratitude on your part and repent immediately.

Let's pray for just one moment:

"Father, forgive us for ingratitude, unthankfulness and *any blindness toward the Harvest* You have provided. It is true that our complaining spirit has robbed us and aborted many miracles You had scheduled for us. In the name of Jesus, I release myself to You. I give all of me to You, knowing that You will reveal wonderful and powerful things to me. Thank You for my *health*, my *eyesight*, and *ability to walk* today. Thank You for the mind that You've given me, and the *doors of favor* that have opened into my life. You are a marvelous, powerful and giving God. *I am thankful.* I am grateful. And I shall not forget Your hand of blessing in my life. Show me what to do. I will obey You. I will listen to Your voice, and I'll be swift to give You the glory and praise for every good thing You do for me. You will receive ten percent of everything You bless me with, and even more as you provide. I *thank you* for every blessing in the name of Jesus. Amen."

❧ 11 ❧

SOME GIVE ONLY WHEN THEY FEEL LIKE IT INSTEAD OF WHEN A MAN OF GOD INSPIRES THEM.

Faith Moments Are Miracle Moments.

You Are Never Closer To God Than When You Sow A Seed Inspired By A Man Of God.

Observe Elijah. He looked into the anguished face of a tormented widow of Zarephath. Can you possibly imagine the depths of sorrow her soul had plunged? She had watched her emaciated son wither and shrivel up before her very eyes. She had taken a long, slow march to a tragedy. Her problem was not a mere broken down automobile. Her problem was not paying her house note on time. Her financial dream wasn't "new clothes." She was one meal away from death.

Is this the kind of crisis that inspires *giving*? Hardly. It is the kind of moment that inspires *hoarding.* You're angry. You're sad. You're hurting. You do not want to hear any preacher discuss "sowing Seed." In fact, any talk about offerings would infuriate and anger anybody in this kind of crisis. It would be normal for her to say to Elijah, "If you had the heart of God, you would be giving to the poor instead of asking for money from me. If you really knew God, you would have brought me a meal, instead of an offering envelope."

She had every reason to question his validity as a man of God. Where was his sensitivity? Where was his compassion, the proof that he cared?

The proof that he cared was his refusal to bog down and wallow with her in sympathy and self-pity. He fueled her faith, not her self-pity. She had every reason to question him, but, she did not. She had something that few have — *the ability to recognize a man of God when he came along.* She had the ability to listen to a challenge instead of criticize it.

When God loves you enough to assign a man of God to unlock your faith, you must recognize it as the moment for your miracle.

I had a puzzling and troubling experience several years ago. It was at one of my World Wisdom Conferences. I will never forget it as long as I live. Someone handed me a note and said, "A minister here feels led to receive an offering for your ministry."

"No, I have already received one. This is not the time," I replied. One of my closest friends, Nancy Harmon, came and stood beside me and whispered.

"Mike, this man really wants to receive an offering. He feels that God has spoken to him specifically at this point to receive an offering."

"No, Nancy. I'm the host here, and I really do not feel God in this at all."

Within a few moments, our evangelist friend came to me. Tears were in his eyes and on his face.

He was shaking his head. "Brother, I'm supposed to receive an offering for your ministry."

It bothered me. It almost agitated and angered me. Nobody wants to be led by the Holy Spirit more than Mike Murdock. I am more sensitive than anybody could imagine. (Anyone who has written over 5,000 songs is sensitive!) I simply did not feel the "wind of God" blowing in *that service* for finances. *I had a different plan* for a special offering later that night and I'd already received an offering earlier.

But, I could not doubt he was a man of God.

His life proved it. *Proven* men of God embraced *him* as a credible evangelist. Thousands had come to Christ through him. He was dynamic. Articulate. He obviously carried the Mantle of financial blessing on his life.

So, I handed him the microphone. I felt as cold as Alaska, but stood quietly nearby. He cried. Everybody else cried. The offering was received. Many people rushed to the front. They were carrying checks for $1,000 and many others came for faith promises. *I never did feel God in it.* Even to this day, as I remember those moments, I never "felt" God in the entire offering. However, everyone else received incredible blessing and happiness. Testimonies have come from that service. Over $100,000 was promised or given to our ministry to buy television time. *Yet, I stood in the presence of the man of God and did not feel anything.*

But, God *required* me to trust His man, whether I felt it or not. Had I refused to trust the challenge of a man of God, my partners would have lost all their Harvests. My ministry would have lost $100,000 to purchase television airtime. Bills would have been unpaid. Oh, I wonder how much has been lost through our unwillingness to accept the man God sends to us.

If you could see how much financial blessing has been lost because of the moments you decided to go by "your feelings," it would sicken your heart. If God was to replay the voice of every man of God He had sent to you, and remind you of your response of unbelief, you would be unable to sleep tonight.

Your heart would be broken.

I was in Tulsa during the month of June, 1994. After a board meeting, I went into a major service. A wonderful minister friend of mine took the microphone and proceeded to receive an offering. Now, I had already given this ministry several thousand dollars. So, I sat calmly as others prepared their offerings. My checkbook was at home (I don't usually like to give cash). I had no intention of giving whatsoever.

Suddenly, the minister instructed, "I want everyone to plant a Seed of $200, every minister here." If I remember correctly, he told us to focus our Seed for a double portion of the presence of God, and a real visitation of the Holy Spirit in our lives. Of course, nothing was even implied that you could buy a miracle from God. Any fool knows you cannot purchase *a miracle* from God with money. Certainly you cannot *buy* the Holy Spirit.

Suddenly my minister friend announced, "While the Holy Spirit is hovering over this place, while the soil is moist, plant your Seed. *Do it now.*"

I had no interest in sowing another Seed. None. I give and give and give. Sometimes, I am simply tired of giving. Especially to a ministry that had received much from me already.

Now, I have a healthy fear of God in my life. It operates strongly. The thought of "missing the will of God" is terrifying to me.

Something touched *my spirit*. I knew it was *important* for me to plant this Seed of $200. So, I reached reluctantly, *but obediently*, and pulled out two $100 bills. I sowed the Seed. And, walked out of the conference and never thought about my Seed again.

But, the Holy Spirit remembered.

Oh, I'm so thankful for the precious Holy Spirit in my life! He has salvaged me from so many crises! He has opened so many golden doors of opportunity! He has created the Golden Connection with so many precious friends! He is your precious Source of Blessing too!

My Harvest came in less than 30 days.

I went to bed at 5:00 a.m. on a Wednesday morning, July 13, 1994. Two hours later, I was awakened by the Holy Spirit. That day was the greatest day in my lifetime of memories. I had an indescribable, an unforgettable encounter with the Holy Spirit on July 13. I would trade every other discovery of my lifetime for what I've discovered about the Holy Spirit on that day. *Less than 30 days* after my Seed of $200... *in obedience to a man of God.* Since then, I have written hundreds of songs to the Holy Spirit, held scores of Schools of the Holy Spirit and watched thousands enter into the greatest season of their spiritual life. The answer was simple.

I had obeyed the instruction of a man of God.

At some point in your life, God will place His servant before you. His servant will look you in the eye and challenge you to plant a Seed of obedience.

> *Some Will Never Receive A Harvest Because They Ignore The Miracle Moment When A Man Of God Inspires Their Faith.*

It will be an *illogical* Seed. It will be a *challenging* Seed.

It will require every ounce of your faith.

If you choose to reject his challenge, you will miss the most glorious Season of Harvest you could have ever tasted.

If you choose to *obey* the man of God, the Golden Door of Blessing will swing wide and you will step *out of famine* into the Season of Prosperity you have desired your entire life.

Let us pray:

"Oh, Father, forgive us for staying in the arena of self-righteousness, logic and human ability. When you bring your servant into our life, it is to bless and empower us. You are a good God, a wonderful God. A giving God. One of the greatest things You do is inspire us to let go of something in our hand so You will let go of what is in Your hand for us. In Jesus' name. Amen."

≈ 12 ≈

MANY ARE NOT WORKING AT THEIR PLACE OF ASSIGNMENT.

Your Assignment Is Always To A Place.

The early disciples knew this very well. "As they ministered to the Lord, and fasted, the Holy Ghost said, Separate me Barnabus and Saul for the work whereunto I have called them" (Acts 13:2).

The Holy Spirit is the only One who knows where your gifts will flourish and where you really belong. "So they, being sent forth by the Holy Ghost departed unto Seleucia; and from thence they sailed to Cyprus" (Acts 13:4).

Philip also knew the importance of obeying the voice of the Holy Spirit to go to a certain place. "And the angel of the Lord spake unto Philip, saying, Arise, and go toward the south unto the way that goeth down from Jerusalem unto Gaza, which is desert. And he arose and went: and, behold, a man of Ethiopia, an eunuch of great authority under Candace queen of the Ethiopians...Was returning, and sitting in his chariot read Esaias the prophet. Then the Spirit said unto Philip, Go near, and join thyself to this chariot" (Acts 8:26-29).

Jesus understood the importance of being in the right place at the right time. "He left Judaea, and departed again unto Galilee. And He must needs go through Samaria" (John 4:3, 4). It was here that He changed the life of the woman of Samaria forever.

▶ *The right people are waiting for you at the right place of Assignment* (Ruth 1-4).

▶ *The right miracles always occur when you are at the right place* (John 6:19-21).

▶ *Prosperity and provision are always available when you are at the right place* (John 6:12, 13).

▶ *Favor always flows toward you when you are laboring at the right place* (Ruth 2:3-18).

It happened to Ruth when Boaz, the wealthy land owner observed her working in his field.

Those you love the most may not discern where you really belong. Ruth experienced this when her embittered mother-in-law insisted she return with her sister-in-law back to Moab instead of following her to Bethlehem. "Behold, thy sister-in-law is gone back unto her people, and unto her gods: return thou after thy sister-in-law" (Ruth 1:15).

Working and saying NO at the right place of your Assignment may require uncommon tenacity and persistence. Naomi saw this in the heart of Ruth when she tried to discourage her from accompanying her to Bethlehem. "When she saw that she was steadfastly minded to go with her, then she left speaking unto her" (Ruth 1:18).

> **You May Have To Exit A Place Of Comfort To Enter A Place Of Promotion.**

You May Have To Exit A Place Of Comfort To Enter A Place Of Promotion. "And Ruth said, Intreat me not to leave thee, or to return from following after thee: for whither thou goest, I will go; and where thou lodgest, I will lodge: thy people shall be my people, and thy God my God: Where thou diest, will I die, and there will I be buried: the Lord do so to me, and more also, if ought but death part thee and me" (Ruth 1:16, 17).

The place that often appears to be the wrong place may become the right place. This may be where you make the Golden Connection of your lifetime. "And Joseph's master took him, and put him into the prison, a place where the king's prisoners were bound: and he was there in the prison. But the Lord was with Joseph, and showed him mercy and gave him favour in the sight of the keeper of the prison" (Genesis 39:20, 21).

It was in this same prison where false accusation placed him that Joseph met the butler *who connected him to Pharaoh.* There, he became the prime minister of all of Egypt. Don't be discouraged today because it appears your dreams and goals will never come to pass.

The greatest friendships are often birthed in very terrible places and difficult circumstances.

Difficult Places Often Turn Out To Be Great Places. "The keeper of the prison looked not to anything that was under his hand; because the Lord was with him, (Joseph) and that which he did, the Lord made it to prosper" (Genesis 39:23).

Geography greatly matters in your success. It is so important to be led by the Holy Spirit. "For as many as are led by the Spirit of God, they are the sons of God" (Romans 8:14). God promises that you'll hear a voice behind you saying "This is the way, walk ye in it" (Isaiah 30:21).

The right place often appears to be the wrong place at first. Joseph discovered this. The prison could not have looked appealing. He did not exclaim, "Yes! Exactly like I saw in my dream!" Hardly. But, it was the place where God was directing his steps. *This is trust.* This reveals confidence in the God of his life. "Trust in the Lord with all thine heart; and lean not unto thine own understanding. In all thy ways acknowledge Him, and He shall direct thy paths" (Proverbs 3:5, 6).

When you are where you really belong, you'll find yourself becoming excited about your work. You even arrive early and often work overtime. Why? You're in the center of your Assignment — the place where you are celebrated instead of tolerated. You will look for *changes* that can improve the environment, *solutions* that solve problems, and continuously find something to improve.

When you are working at the wrong place, you may habitually start arriving late. Subconsciously, you are dreading getting there. You wait 15 minutes ahead of time at the punch-out clock anxious to leave for home. You complain and gripe about every little change that occurs. You work slower than everyone else. Your mistakes increase because of your inability to focus. Attentiveness becomes impossible.

You are simply at the wrong place or have a wrong attitude towards it.

It is so easy to understand why many people never receive promotions, an extra bonus or a raise. They are *not* where they should be. Their lack of desire for excellence is proof.

What should you do when you realize you are out of place? Wrong job? Or, you are not fulfilling the center of your Assignment?

First, *recognize that the Holy Spirit may have you there for reasons you may not understand.* Things may be difficult but you can still be the catalyst for change. Titus received this special and unique word from the Apostle Paul. Paul recognized that "The Cretians are always liars, evil beasts, slow bellies" (Titus 1:12). He agreed that the witness was true (Titus 1:13). But, he explained this to Titus, *"For this cause left I thee in Crete,* that thou shouldest set in order the things that are wanting, and ordain elders in every city, as I had appointed thee... Wherefore rebuke them sharply, that they may be sound in the faith; Not giving heed to Jewish fables, and commandments of men, that turn from the truth" (Titus 1:5, 13, 14).

Your Assignment will never be to someone who is perfect or you would have no place to go.

Your Assignment will not always be to a perfect environment; you may be the one assigned to bring it to a new level of excellence.

Wherever you are presently assigned, determine to excel. As you do, you will receive the special attention of God. "Servants, be obedient to them that are your masters according to the flesh, with fear and trembling, in singleness of your heart, as unto Christ; Not with eyeservice, as men pleasers; but as the servants of Christ, doing the will of God from the heart" (Ephesians 6:5, 6).

Your aim should be the highest level of excellence because you are doing it unto God and not simply to your boss. "With good will doing service, as to the Lord, and not to men" (Ephesians 6:7).

Whatever you do to excel (even in your present position) will be honored, compensated and fully rewarded by the God who observes you continually. "Knowing that whatsoever good thing any man doeth, the same shall he receive of the Lord, whether he be bond or free" (Ephesians 6:8). It is a powerful Golden Key that I have used countless hundreds of time in my life: What You Make Happen For Others, God Will Make Happen For You. Do your work with such excellence that your standard excels and surpasses that of your co-workers.

Exceed your supervisor's expectations so that you are chosen to replace him. "And the keeper of the prison committed to Joseph's hand all the prisoners that were in the prison; and whatsoever they did there, he was the doer of it" (Genesis 39:22).

Continuously explore opportunities to solve uncommon problems. Joseph did. "And Joseph came in unto them in the morning, and looked upon them, and, behold, they were sad" (Genesis 40:6). It was this keen observation and the attentiveness to the problems of others that brought Joseph to the Golden Door of the palace. When he accurately interpreted the dreams of the butler and the baker, he created a corridor to the heart of Pharaoh.

Interpreting dreams was not on his job resume. Nobody else had discerned this gift within him. He alone knew his gift and calling. *He continuously looked for an opportunity for God to use them.* Within 24 months he was the prime minister of the greatest nation on earth, Egypt.

Uncommon diligence always attracts attention.

Do your work with such diligence that you become the topic of conversation of others. This happened to Ruth. Boaz asked his servants, "Whose damsel is this?" She was so diligent they discussed her incredible schedule of work, "She came, and hath continued even from the morning until now, that she tarried a little in the house" (Ruth 2:7).

Financial crisis can make you vulnerable. Maybe you accepted the most convenient or accessible job opportunity available. Deep in your heart you have become frustrated and discontented. Your greatest gifts are lying dormant. Undiscovered. Undiscerned. Unused. *Unrewarded.*

Oh, I want to encourage you today! *Seasons will change.* You will not stay where you are very long. Using the Golden Key of Diligence (speedy attention to an assigned task) and Integrity (doing exactly what you promised your boss you would do on the schedule he expected) you will rise above it all.

Many years ago, I read that seven out of ten employees in America were working on the wrong jobs, performing tasks they dreaded and never receiving a promotion because of it.

That's one of the major reasons you may not be receiving the financial Harvest God wants you to enjoy.

I will never forget the conversation. After I spoke one evening, an older man walked up to me and complained, "Dr. Mike, this prosperity stuff never worked for me."

"Well, tell me about it," I replied.

"I've worked on my job 27 years."

"You must love your job, " I admired.

"I hate my job," was his surprising reply.

"Well, then why are your working there?" I asked.

His reply should be carved in concrete. I will never forget it as long as I live.

"It is only ten minutes from my house."

I stared in disbelief. Convenience had made a slave out of an incredible potential champion.

Then, he added another shocking statement that explained why he stayed on the same job for 27 long dreary years.

"In three years, I will get a gold watch." Imagine exchanging one half of your working life for a little gold watch. How tragic!

Are you working on your job because it's *near your house?* Are you working at your job because the demands are few? Have you really spent time in the Secret Place, inquiring of the Holy Spirit as to the place where you should empty your life? Is it serious enough to you to enter a special time of *fasting?* Are you working at your job because it appears to pay more money than where you really belong? Does this indicate that you can be "bought" if the money is right?

"Well, you know, a man has got to eat, Dr. Mike." Is that your major goal in life, to have just enough money for survival?

Provision Is Only Guaranteed At Your Place Of Obedience. Ruth had to be at the place where Boaz could see her. Joseph had to be seen by Pharaoh before he was promoted.

If you never want to go to work early, I would start questioning if I

> **Provision Is Only Guaranteed At Your Place Of Obedience.**

were really at the right place.

If you never have a passion to stay late and complete a project, I would ask the question to make certain I was at the right place of Assignment.

If you are at the place where God has *presently* assigned you, *give your best.* Stop looking across the fence at "greener grass." Make your present responsibilities your total focus. Become obsessed with achieving the highest level of excellence any one has ever reached in your position.

If you are *not* where God has assigned you, start moving. Talk it out with your mentor, your boss and your family. Find out where you would excel and do your very very best.

When you are at the right place, the right people move toward you.

One Day Of Favor Is Worth A Thousand Days Of Labor. You cannot work hard enough to get everything you deserve or want. You cannot work enough jobs to create everything you want. You must move in the currents of uncommon favor.

Uncommon favor only occurs when you are where God has assigned you.

When you are where you belong, you will love what you do. You will not require the constant encouragement and motivation from others. Instead you will excite those around you.

When you are where you belong, there will be a natural joy that creates an incredible environment of motivation for others.

An intriguing story occurs in 1 Kings 17. The prophet Elijah is commanded to go to the brook Cherith. There he finds his miracle of provision during the famine. A raven feeds him daily, and the brook supplies his water. *He was where he belonged.*

Suddenly, a crisis occurs. The brook dried up. The raven did not return with food. Why? His place of Assignment had *changed.*

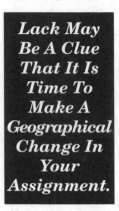

Lack May Be A Clue That It Is Time To Make A Geographical Change In Your Assignment.

Lack May Be A Clue That It Is Time To Make A Geographical Change In Your Assignment.

Jesus instructed Peter to go fishing. When he caught the fish, a coin for tax money was in its mouth. Why? He was where he had been assigned.

When you are at your place of Assignment, you will notice things others may overlook. A tailor notices a missing button. The hair stylist sees the roots of the hair need dying again. The mechanic hears a sound in your car engine nobody else heard.

Your Assignment determines *the problems* that *get your attention.* This occurred in Joseph's life. He noticed the sad countenance of two prisoners, the butler and the baker. Joseph responded and it was the vital link to his promotion.

When you are at the wrong place, you may often overlook problems that you should solve.

When you are at the right place, you may be more discerning and intuitive than everyone else around you. Why? You are at the place of your Assignment. Nobody is seeing what you see, knows what you know or cares as much as you care.

Someone asked me once, "What are the major differences you see between the wealthy and the poor?"

I answered, "When I talk to the poor, they are

always doing something they hate. But, when I talk to the wealthy, they are always doing projects and *things they really love.* When I talk to the poor, they are anxious to get home from work. When I talk to the wealthy, their passion is like a magnet keeping them at their place of business."

Somebody said it so well: "If you love your work, you will never really work a single day in your life." Oh, how true!

Stop and evaluate your life today. Do not keep rushing into a future you have not gazed upon. Do not amble and wonder aimlessly through life. Life is too precious to throw away.

What topic would you rather discuss than any other topic on earth? What books do you love to read? If you could write a book about any subject, what would it be? These are clues to your life Assignment.

Many never find where they really belong and consequently never receive the financial Harvests their heavenly Father is longing to give to them.

∽ 2 Samuel 24:25 ∽

"And David built there an altar unto the Lord, and offered burnt offerings and peace offerings. So the Lord was intreated for the land, and the plague was stayed from Israel."

☙ 13 ☙

Most People Have Never Learned The Secret Of Giving Their Seed A Specific Assignment.

Every Seed Contains An Invisible Instruction.
Let me explain. You cannot see it. It is too small and invisible to the natural eye. But, it is obviously there. If you could look deep into the watermelon Seed, you would see an invisible instruction to "produce a watermelon." Tomato Seeds contain invisible instructions to "produce tomatoes."

There is no wavering or uncertainty. Every Seed contains an incredible Assignment. It is precise, exact and specific. The Creator had decided the Harvest when He created the Seed.

When God wanted a family, He sowed His Son. He gave His Son an Assignment to "seek and save that which was lost." Jesus was the best Seed God ever planted on earth. But, He contained an Assignment, an instruction, a purpose. Everything He did was connected to that Assignment every day of His life.

David tapped into this incredible secret of giving

his Seed a specific Assignment. When thousands lay dead across the city, he cried out to God and *brought Him a specific offering for a specific purpose.* "And David built there an altar unto the Lord, and offered burnt offerings and peace offerings. So the Lord was intreated for the land." What was the Harvest? "And the plague was stayed from Israel" (Read 2 Samuel 24:25).

Elijah taught this incredible Principle of Assignment to the widow of Zarephath. As she was going to bring water, he gave her a specific instruction... "Bring me, I pray thee, a morsel of bread in thine hand."

Then, he did something few ministers ever do. *He gave her a photograph of what her Seed was going to produce.* "For thus saith the Lord God of Israel, The barrel of meal shall not waste, neither shall the cruse of oil fail, until the day that the Lord sendeth rain upon the earth" (1 Kings 17:14).

When you give your Seed an Assignment, incredible faith pours into you. You can see beyond the sacrifice of the moment. The widow did. "And she went and did according to the saying of Elijah: and she, and he, and her house, did eat many days" (1 Kings 17:15).

Does it really work? If you sow for a specific reason, toward a Harvest, does it work? It works *if you are doing it in total obedience to the instructions of God.* "And the barrel of meal wasted not, neither did the cruse of oil fail, according to the word of the Lord, which he spake by Elijah" (1 Kings 17:16). Those instructions may be through a servant of God, the Word of God or through the inner voice of the Holy Spirit.

Your prayers are Seeds, too.

Job *sowed a prayer of deliverance* for his three friends. What happened? God turned Job's captivity around! Just like David had stopped a tragedy by offering a special offering to the Lord.

Many years ago, I experienced a personal attack. It was devastating to me emotionally. My mind was fragmented. Inside, my heart was broken, and I wanted to die. It was a situation that would have been complicated by any retaliation or attempts of explanation. I flew to Los Angeles for another crusade on the same day. The next morning, a Sunday, the Holy Spirit gave me a strange instruction. "Plant a battle Seed."

I had never heard of such a thing. When you want something you've never had, you've got to do something you have never done.

Then, I remembered when David had *aimed his Seed like an arrow.* He gave it an Assignment. He focused it for a desired result. And the plague was stayed (2 Samuel 24:25).

I planted everything I had that day — $3,000. Supernaturally the attack ended as suddenly as it had began. Isn't that wonderful? You always have a Seed that becomes an exit from your present circumstances.

Your Seed is always the door out of trouble. It is anything you do that *helps* another person. Your Seed is anything that *improves the life* of someone near you. It may be the Seed of information, Seed of encouragement or even the Seed of finances. Whatever you plant, you must remember to give your Seed a specific Assignment so that your faith will not waver. "But let him ask in faith, nothing wavering. For he that wavereth is like a wave of the sea driven with the wind and tossed. For let not that man think that he shall receive anything of the Lord. A double-minded man is unstable in all his ways" (James 1:6-8).

Your faith must have a specific instruction. Not two. Not three. One. "This one thing I do," was the words of the great man of God. David cried out, "My heart is fixed" (Psalm 57:7).

Don't waver. Aim your Seed. "Turn not from it to the right hand nor to the left, that thou mayest prosper whithersoever thou goest" (Joshua 1:7).

The Only Reason Men Fail Is Broken Focus.

Giving your Seed a specific Assignment strongly impacts your focus. And focus matters. The secret of success is concentration. The Only Reason Men Fail Is Broken Focus.

It is a tragic situation that I have observed on many Sunday mornings in churches. The offering is being received. The pastor explains how the offering will be spent, "We really need a roof. The present roof is in need of repair. Will you help us today?"

The people respond. But their Seed has not really received an instruction. Of course it pays the bills. But, it does not really multiply back into their lives. Why? It has not been aimed to create a specific Harvest or desired result. You see, if the only desired result involved is to pay the roofer, that is accomplished easily...but the Seed sowers never receive their personal Harvest in return. Sow your Seed *consistently. Generously.* And always in *obedience* to the voice of God. Then, wrap your faith around your Seed and target it like an arrow. Enter into a covenant for a specific and desired result in your life.

Thousands fail to do this and never enjoy the financial Harvest God promised. "Ye have not, because ye ask not" (James 4:2).

Let's pray together:

"Father, you gave Jesus, your best Seed, an Assignment. You wanted a Family. Now, millions are born again and changed forever. You are producing the Harvest you desired. Teach us the Principle of Assignment — giving every Seed we sow, a specific Assignment. Remind us to water and nurture this Seed with expectation, doubting nothing. In Jesus' name. Amen."

❧ Ecclesiastes 5:4,5 ❧

"When thou vowest a vow unto God, defer
not to pay it; for He hath no pleasure in
fools: pay that which thou has vowed.
Better is it that thou shouldest not vow,
that thou should vow and not pay."

❧ 14 ❧

MANY FORGET OR REFUSE TO PAY THEIR VOWS MADE TO GOD.

Vows Are Not Frivolous Things To God.
God is not playful, frivolous nor trivial.

He takes your promises to Him quite seriously. "When thou vowest a vow unto God, defer not to pay it; for he hath no pleasures in fools: pay that which thou has vowed. Better is it that thou shouldest not vow, that thou should vow and not pay" (Ecclesiastes 5:4, 5).

God describes promise breakers as fools. That's why it is so important not to position yourself as a fool because fools are ultimately destroyed.

God humiliates fools.

God moves away from fools.

God uses fools as illustrations for destruction.

Always keep your promises. To your family. To your wife or husband. To the Lord who promised you His best. It is important that you develop impeccable and unwavering integrity when you give your word in a business transaction or to your children.

God is a covenant God. He remembers every vow you have made before Him and man.

Oh, stop and re-examine your life this very moment! Have you made any financial vows to your church or to the man of God in your life? Pay them. Whatever it takes. *Pay your vows.*

It will break "the curse." When you keep your vow, God's very best begins to come to you. Read Deuteronomy 28 and Leviticus 26. God guarantees that incredible blessings always come to those who "observe and to do all His commandments" (Deuteronomy 28:1).

After an anointed banquet one evening, an articulate and well-dressed lady approached me.

"I know God has spoken to me tonight to plant a Seed of $1,000 in your ministry. You will receive it in a few days," she said wiping tears of joy from her eyes.

A few days later, her letter arrived. It was an apology. "After I talked to my husband, I felt that I should break my promise to you. I do not believe we can really afford to sow this special Seed at this time," she wrote. Oh, the heartache that broken promises are creating in our lives.

You see, *while she was in the presence of God* and the anointing of the Holy Spirit was hovering over the congregation, *the Seeds of her faith exploded within her heart.*

God spoke.

She heard.

She moved swiftly.

She quickly declared her covenant with God. After she moved *away* from His presence, discussed this gigantic step of faith with *an unbelieving* husband, she *withdrew* from her covenant which she had entered into with God. Oh, only time will reveal the curse that such an attitude of frivolity and lightheartedness will produce in our lives.

Many years ago I was sitting in my bed watching a religious television program. Suddenly, a famous evangelist looked into the camera and said so forcibly, "If you have made a vow to God at any time and not paid it, you have launched a parade of tragedies. Please sit down today and pay your vows."

Conviction smote my heart.

Over two years before, I had promised a missionary in Africa that I would help sponsor some students for scholarships in his Bible college. I had asked him to rush me material about it. When I did not receive the material, I did nothing. I did not telephone him or pursue a reason. I simply used it as an excuse to "escape my vow" that I had made to him.

As I watched the telecast that night, God reminded me of my promise. As I felt my heart pound, I knelt beside my bed and prayed, "Please forgive me. Give me another chance. Do not withhold your Harvest from me." It was midnight, but I called my secretary anyway. "Whatever you do, when you arrive at the office tomorrow morning, please take the checkbook. Write out a check to this Bible school in East Africa. Airmail it. I cannot live another day without the blessing of God flowing upon me. I cannot afford a curse in my life and ministry."

I have seen hundreds lift their hands and make faith promises, "Yes, I will plant a monthly Seed to help you spread the Wisdom of God." Yet, over 50 percent will never sit down and plant that Seed of Promise they vowed publicly to plant.

"Maybe they cannot afford to do it!" is a common explanation.

I have seen many people make this claim, yet

they continue to receive salary raises, new television sets, and purchase a new automobile. They take their family out to eat at the nicest restaurants, purchase new clothes and send their children through college. Throughout all of this spending, they make the same claim, "I really cannot keep my faith promise."

"Would you like for me to ask God to make you as poor as you tell everybody you really are?" I asked jokingly of one of my relatives one day.

When you make a faith promise, you've entered into a covenant between you and God. Don't treat it lightly and with frivolity. Make every effort to pay it.

If you do not presently have enough finances to fully pay your vow at one time, start planting small Seeds *as often as possible.* Your Harvest will start increasing. Then, you will find it possible to *complete* your faith promise and vow and begin your days of Blessing.

Do you truly feel that you have made a mistake? Then ask the Lord to give you an extra supernatural miracle so that you can complete your faith vow to Him in a supernatural way. *You are only responsible with what He provides.* If He does not provide, you are released of your part.

It is not merely the man of God who is authorized necessarily to *"let you off."* This faith promise is between you and God. It must be settled between you and Him.

An unpaid vow is one of the powerful reasons thousands have never tasted the reward of their step of faith.

Let's pray together:

"Father, forgive me for any unpaid vows. You

will come first from this day on. I will keep my covenant with you because *I need the Harvest far more than I need my Seed.* Provide for me and make it possible for me to have the finances necessary to keep my word. You know my heart of faith and will not disappoint me. I believe your Word today. In Jesus' name. Amen."

∾ Proverbs 11:14 ∾

"Where no counsel is, the people fall: but in the multitude of counselors there is safety."

 15

Many Are Unwilling To Patiently Sit At The Feet Of A Financial Mentor.

What You Keep Hearing You Eventually Believe. You must treasure every moment you have access to a qualified Mentor.

What you don't respect will move away from you. It may be a miracle, a dog, or money. But there are currents in life just like there are currents in air and water. These currents move you toward your dreams or away from them; toward success or failure; toward prosperity or poverty.

> **When God Hears The Cry Of The Captive, He Assigns A Deliverer To His Life.**

What you respect will move toward you. It may be people, or money.

When God wants to bless you, He puts a person in your life.

Moses was assigned to be the Deliverer who led the Israelites out of their bondage in Egypt. Those who respected his leadership found their bondage broken, and headed toward Canaan, the land of promise.

Elijah was a Deliverer. God took him away from

the privacy of the brook, Cherith, and sent him to the home of a starving widow. The town was Zarephath. Her son was one meal from death. But, God sent her a man *who was not intimidated by her poverty.* This prophet carried the mantle to unlock her faith for a supernatural financial Harvest.

▶ If you are spiritually lost, you must begin to look for the man of God who has focused his life to bring the salvation message to the unbeliever.

▶ If you are sick, you must look for and respect the man of God who carries the mantle and anointing for divine healing and health.

▶ If you are facing financial problems and bankruptcy, start looking for the man or woman of God who carries the mantle of Financial Breakthrough.

You see, what you respect will move toward you. When you respect and celebrate the financial mantle of those God sends into your life, prosperity will explode like a Niagara Falls across your life.

Nobody fails alone.

If you fail or experience financial devastation, it could well be because you chose to ignore a man of God assigned to help you unlock the treasures and unleash your financial faith.

Your Mentors must be recognized and pursued.

Jesus reached out to help and was ignored. You can almost feel the tears flowing down His cheeks as He cried, "O Jerusalem, Jerusalem, thou that killest the prophets, and stonest them which are sent unto thee, how often would I have gathered thy children together, even as a hen gathereth her chickens under her wings, and ye would not! Behold, your house is left unto you desolate" (Matthew 23:37, 38).

Your Mentors can upgrade your financial decisions. If you can make the decisions that create your poverty, then you can make decisions that can create your prosperity. If you can do something that brings decrease, you can learn to do the things that create increase.

▶ You must discern the *Financial Mentors* closest to you.

▶ You must learn to celebrate the *Financial Deliverers* God has made accessible to you.

Reaching is a requirement.

Reaching out for financial Wisdom and assistance is not a sign of weakness. Only a fool ignores a life jacket when he is drowning. Those who overcome financial devastation never do it alone. They conquer their pride. They reject the trap of isolation. They know the inevitable reward for reaching.

"Whatever You Are Most Thankful For Will Increase In Your Life." (Quote from Sherman Owens.)

They pursue.

They ask.

You must turn to God first. Become thankful for what He has already given to you in your life.

First, *be thankful* for His previous provision and supernatural supply.

Express gratitude for those who have assisted you in achieving your dream, given you job opportunities, and encouraged you.

Your heavenly Father cares

about your financial difficulties today. You really do matter to Him. Jesus said it clearly, "Your heavenly Father knoweth that ye have need of all these things" (Matthew 6:32).

He is expecting your pursuit of Him. In the Secret Place of prayer. In the church services that you attend. In your diligent research of Scripture. "When thou art in tribulation, and all these things are come upon thee, even in the latter days, if thou turn to the Lord thy God, and shalt be obedient unto His voice; (For the Lord thy God is a merciful God;) He will not forsake thee, neither destroy thee, nor forget the covenant of thy fathers which He sware unto them" (Deuteronomy 4:30, 31).

Nobody else can do it for you. Nobody else feels your pain. Nobody else is staring at the stack of bills you are facing every night.

Pursue worthy and proven counsel. Somebody knows something you need to know. Someone knows something that can help you survive and even succeed in the middle of the most painful chapter of your life. Ignorance is too costly. It is deadly.

Only fools risk the consequences of ignorance.

Your pastor, or boss, or someone you love may have a recommendation of a certified financial planner or others in your area. Whatever you do today, take the time to listen to godly advice. True champions do. As the ancient writings teach, "Where no counsel is, the people fall: but in the multitude of counselors there is safety" (Proverbs 11:14).

God expects you to cry out for help in times of trouble. "This poor man cried, and the Lord heard him, and saved him out of all his troubles" (Psalm 34:6).

Your humility and desperation will attract God. Especially your faith. You must trust God to stop the financial attack against you. You serve a very capable and caring God. He can turn the hearts of kings in favor toward you.

You are on His mind this very moment. Your tears, your pain, and your fears affect Him and influence His responses to you. He is getting ready to move in your behalf. Trust Him. Regardless of the storms around you, remember the great promise, "He maketh wars to cease..." (Psalm 46:9).

Recognize messengers who carry the message of financial solutions. They may be packaged like a John the Baptist in a loin cloth of camel's hair, or the silk robes like King Solomon. Don't permit the packaging to distract you from the message. They may appear arrogant, cocky and self-confident. Or, they may seem humble, timid and even reluctant to share their financial knowledge. It is your responsibility to discern the messengers God sends into your life. Drop your pail in their well.

Your response to a man of God is carefully documented by God.

When God talks to you, it is often through the spiritual leaders in your life. Don't ignore them. Remember — "He that receiveth a prophet in the name of a prophet shall receive a prophet's reward; and he that receiveth a righteous man in the name of a righteous man shall a receive a righteous man's reward" (Matthew 10:41).

Recognize extraordinary and uncommon Mentors of Faith. You see, your faith determines the flow of miracles toward you. "But without faith, it is impossible to please Him" (Hebrews 11:6).

"He that cometh unto God must believe that He is and that He is a rewarder of them that diligently seek Him" (Hebrews 11:6).

Moses mentored Joshua.

Paul mentored Timothy.

Elijah mentored Elisha.

Naomi mentored Ruth.

Mordecai mentored Esther.

Uncommon champions have uncommon mentors. Observe carefully the lives of those who have succeeded around you. Their secrets will begin to surface. Their reason for unusual success will become quite clear. Study the biographies of financial champions. Extraordinary people have tapped into the fountain of their faith. As you read their journey from the pit to the palace, you'll be encouraged and strengthened. "Wherefore seeing we also are compassed about with so great a cloud of witnesses, let us lay aside every weight, and the sin which doth so easily beset us, and let us run with patience the race that is set before us" (Hebrews 12:1).

Constantly eat faith food. What you read will affect what you believe.

What you read influences the conversations you enter.

When you feed the Word of God into your spirit man, your faith (confidence in God) comes alive and becomes a living force within you.

Set aside a specific time every day to read three chapters in the Bible. Nurture and grow the explosive Seeds of faith within you. Acorns can become oak trees. "So then faith cometh by hearing, and hearing by the word of God" (Romans 10:17).

Choose a proven mentor. Those you admire will eternally affect your future. Choose financial mentors who increase your faith in the true Source, God. Learn from their *scars* as well as their *sermons.* "And we beseech you, brethren, to know them which labour among you, and are over you in the Lord, and admonish you; And to esteem them very highly in love for their work's sake" (1 Thessalonians 5:12, 13).

Financial Mentors are different than Financial Deliverers. Mentors impart expertise. Deliverers create experiences. *You need both.*

Your mentor takes you on a *continuous journey* from where you are to the place you can be. This involves a collection of instructions, a series of crises and constant review of your financial situation.

A financial deliverer carries a mantle and an anointing that *breaks the spirit of poverty* over your life and unlocks a financial faith never experienced before.

➤ Somebody gave you instructions that created your present circumstances.

➤ Somebody must give you different instructions to create the circumstances that you desire. "Poverty and shame comes to him that refuseth instruction" (Proverbs 13:18).

Many rebel against any correction or advice given to them. This is the reason they never taste the incredible Harvest God wants them to have.

Several years ago, I had a close friend I loved and admired very much. Something agitated him and he quit attending a special weekly Bible study that I held. His house was just minutes away. A few months later, he began to experience tremendous financial loses. One day, I met his wife in a store.

"You've got to pray for my husband. He's almost

bankrupt." Her face looked so pulled and stressed.

"Well, he ought to be in bad shape," I said half jesting but really serious. "He has refused to drive ten minutes to sit under a financial mantle of a financial deliverer where God is pouring out financial blessing. He has ignored and disregarded the access he has had to this anointing."

Sometimes that which becomes familiar becomes hidden to us.

Someone I love was very concerned about a close relative. "Unless there is a miracle, they are going to go bankrupt."

"You know," I replied, "every Thursday night I teach from the Word of God on the Laws of Financial Supply. They could sit under this mantle within minutes if they would make the drive. They have refused to sit under this anointing." Their financial crisis was not a mystery to me at all.

What you ignore will move away from you.

I have relatives who can hardly earn their own living. They constantly borrow from other relatives. Some would call them parasites, because they cannot earn their own way. Yet, they refuse to sit for three days in a conference that would connect them to the golden flow of supply and the uncommon walk of faith.

No, it is not a shock and surprise to me that many people never experience Harvest. Some will sit an hour in a car on the freeway during a traffic jam every single day of their life, but become angry if their pastor discusses financial Harvest during the offering for more than fifteen minutes.

Think about this. Every week contains 168 hours, or 672 compartments of 15 minutes. If you only sit and receive faith teaching on a capsule of 15 minutes out of the 672, is it any wonder why your faith is not alive and vibrant?

"A wise man will hear, and will increase learning; and a man of understanding shall attain unto wise counsels" (Proverbs 1:5).

What You Hear Is The Only Thing You Can Become.

You must start moving toward extraordinary people. Make a habit of pursuing greatness. Pay any price. Purchase any book or tape series that contains the path to the uncommon supply.

Elisha received a double portion of God's power because he was willing to pay the cost to stay in the presence of Elijah, the great prophet. Joshua observed Moses. Ruth reached for Boaz.

You will never possess what you are unwilling to pursue. You really have no right for anything you have not reached toward. "He that walketh with wise men shall be wise: but a companion of fools shall be destroyed" (Proverbs 13:20).

I was in South Carolina giving my testimony about the Seed of $58, the Covenant of Blessing. This is what I shared: I was in Washington, DC, sitting on the platform. The pastor was receiving the tithe and offerings from his people. Suddenly, the Holy Spirit spoke to me and impressed me to plant a Seed of $58 to represent each of the $58 kinds of blessing in the Bible. It sounded so crazy to me, but I knew the voice of the Holy Spirit. So, I pulled out my checkbook and wrote a check for $58. Then, I felt impressed to plant one for my son who was 12 at the time. My divorce had been bitter. It was difficult to get any time of visitation, and so forth.

Within a few weeks after my Seed, his mother decided he could come spend the rest of his life with me! The miracle flow started. After I shared this in South Carolina. It was interesting the paths that two different people in that service took.

One man called the pastor very upset. He insisted that I was a fraud, trying to con people out of $58. Here was a man who could not discern a financial anointing, a financial deliverer God had sent into his life to unlock his faith. Perhaps, he had some terrible experiences or heard great criticism of ministers in his youthful days. Chances are that his backslidden state from God made him angry at any discussion of money. At any rate, he reacted, and refused to participate in the Seed of $58.

Across the building set another precious lady, a minister of the gospel. Her heart was stirred. She discerned the atmosphere of heaven in the service. She pulled out her checkbook and sowed a special Seed of $58. (On the left-hand side of the check, she wrote "Covenant of Blessing.") A few months later, an old man she had been caring for died. Thinking he was broke, she had been purchasing his medicine for him. She thought he died impoverished. However, after his death, he left her a church paid for, two homes and 27 acres of ground completely paid for! Within two years, the geological report came back that they had discovered gold on the 27 acres of ground!

Same service. Two people.

One sneered and refused to recognize the anointing of God.

The second tasted the supernatural supply.

One man told me after a service one night, "I don't really understand about this Seed of $58."

"It's quite simple. The Seed that leaves your hand never really leaves your life — it simply leaves your hand and goes into your own future where it multiplies."

When You Let Go Of What Is In Your Hand, God Will Let Go Of What Is In His Hand For You.

Those who doubt are forced to live with the consequences of their unbelief. Those who believe can expect to face the rewards of their believing.

Doubt is a tragic and unfortunate cancer in the body of Christ. Oh, precious friend, *don't permit it to destroy your life.*

Some are intimidated by the *self-confidence of a financial deliverer.* To them, financial blessing is a difficult, hard and arduous journey up the long mountain of life. It seems impossible to achieve. When they see the brash and light approach, they're turned off.

Some are thinking about the limitations of their salary instead of hearing about the potential of their faith.

Others simply feel that the risk of the faith life is too great. They hold on to every cent. They hoard. They feel personally responsible for every dollar that comes into their life and cannot grasp the greatness of a Provider, God, who cares deeply for them.

Thousands refuse to embrace the faith challenge of a financial deliverer and mentor that God sends. They will spend the rest of their life scraping pennies, wishing their life could have a breakthrough.

≈ Luke 6:38 ≈

"Give, and it shall be given unto you, good
measure, pressed down, and shaken
together, and running over, shall men give
into your bosom."

～ 16 ～

MANY HAVE NEVER BEEN TAUGHT TO SOW WITH AN EXPECTATION OF A RETURN.

You Can Only Do What You Know.

Thousands have been taught that it is wrong to expect something in return when you give to God.

They feel that this is proof of greed.

"When I give to God, I expect nothing in return!" is the prideful claim of many who have been trapped by tragic and erroneous teaching.

Do you expect a salary from your boss at the end of a work week? Of course, you do. Is this greed? Hardly.

Did you expect forgiveness when you confessed your sins to Christ? Of course, you did. Is this greed? Hardly.

Stripping Expectation From Your Seed Is Theft of The Only Pleasure God Knows.

Stripping Expectation From Your Seed Is Theft Of The *Only Pleasure God Knows.*

Remember, His greatest pleasure is to be believed. His greatest pain is to be doubted. "But without faith, it is impossible to please Him: For he that cometh to God must believe that

He is, and that He is a rewarder... *that He is a rewarder*... of them that diligently seek Him" (Hebrews 11:6).

Motive means *your reason for doing something*.

When someone is on trial accused of murder, prosecutors try to find the possible motive or reason why he should have been motivated to do such a horrible thing.

God Promised You A Harvest To Motivate You To Sow A Seed.	He *expected* you to be motivated by *supply,* the promise of *provision*. "Give, and it shall be given unto you; good measure, pressed down, and shaken together, and running over, shall men give into your bosom" (Luke 6:38). (This is much more than a principle of mercy and forgiveness. This is a Principle in Supply.)

He offers overflow as a reason you should sow Seed! Seeds of forgiveness or whatever you need.

"Honour the Lord with thy substance, and with the firstfruits of all thine increase: So shall thy barns be filled with plenty, and thy presses shall burst out with new wine" (Proverbs 3:9, 10). Notice that God paints the picture of *overflowing barns* to motivate us (give us a reason) for honoring Him.

He promised benefits to those who might be fearful about tithing. "Bring ye all the tithes into the storehouse, that there may be meat in Mine house, and prove Me now herewith, saith the Lord of hosts, if I will not open you the windows of heaven, and pour you out a blessing, that there shall not be room enough to receive it" (Malachi 3:10).

Read Deuteronomy 28:1-14. Here in the

Scripture God creates a list of the specific blessings that will occur *if you obey Him*. Why does He give us these Portraits of Prosperity? *To inspire you and give you a reason to obey.*

Peter needed this kind of encouragement just like you and I do today. He felt such emptiness as he related to Christ that he and the others had "given up everything."

Jesus *promised him a one hundredfold return.* "Then Peter began to say unto Him, Lo, we have left all, and have followed Thee. And Jesus answered and said, Verily I say unto you, There is no man that hath left house, or brethren, or sisters, or father, or mother, or wife, or children, or lands, for My sake, and the gospel's, But he shall receive an hundredfold now in this time, houses, and brethren, and sisters, and mothers, and children, and lands, with persecutions; and in the world to come eternal life" (Mark 10:28-30).

Reaping Is The Reason For Sowing.

Many people think this is evil to sow for a Harvest. *That is the reason to sow!*

Giving is the cure for greed, not hoarding.

When you sow to get a Harvest, you have just mastered greed.

Greed *hoards.*

Man *withholds.*

Satan *steals.*

The nature of God alone is the giving nature. When you give, you have just revealed the nature of God is inside you.

The only pleasure God receives is through acts of faith. I stress this again. His *only* need is to be believed. His *greatest* need is to be believed. "God is not a man that He should lie" (Numbers 23:19).

If an unbeliever confesses to a pastor after church, "I want to give my heart to Christ, pastor." The pastor prays. Suppose the unbeliever then says, "Will you pray that God will give me peace and forgiveness for my confession?"

Imagine a pastor who would reply with indignation — "Of course not! That's greedy. You want something back for giving your heart to Christ?" You would be shocked if your pastor said this.

Your Father offers Supply for Seed; forgiveness for confession; order for chaos.

When Jesus talked to the woman at the well of Samaria, He promised her water that she would never thirst again. Was He wrong to offer her something if she pursued Him? Of course not. That was the purpose of the portrait of water — to motivate her and *give her a reason for obeying Him.*

One day, my dear friend Dwight Thompson, the powerful evangelist, told me a story about the papaya. Somebody counted 470 papaya Seeds in a single papaya. If that was consistent, one papaya Seed will produce a plant containing ten papayas. If each of the ten papayas contained 470 Seeds, there would be 4,700 papaya Seeds on one plant.

Now, just suppose you replant those 4,700 Seeds to create 4,700 more plants. Do you know how much 5,000 plants containing 5,000 Seeds would be? *Twenty five million Seeds...on the second planting alone.*

And we are having troubles really believing in the hundredfold return. Why?

Millions must *unlearn* the poisonous and

traitorous teaching that it is wrong to expect anything in return.

Expectation Is The Powerful Current That Makes The Seed Work For You. "But without faith it is impossible to please Him: for he that cometh to God must believe that He is, and that He is a rewarder of them that diligently seek Him" (Hebrews 11:6).

Expect protection as He promised. "And I will rebuke the devourer for your sakes, and he shall not destroy the fruits of your ground; neither shall your vine cast her fruit before the time in the field, saith the Lord of hosts" (Malachi 3:11).

Expect favor from a Boaz close to you. "Give, and it shall be given unto you; good measure pressed down, and shaken together, and running over, shall men give into your bosom. For with the same measure that ye mete withal it shall be measured to you again" (Luke 6:38).

Expect financial ideas and Wisdom from God as a Harvest. "But thou shalt remember the Lord thy God: for it is He that giveth thee power to get wealth," (Deuteronomy 8:18).

Expect your enemies to fragment and be confused and flee before you. "The Lord shall cause thine enemies that rise up against thee to be smitten before thy face: they shall come out against thee one way, and flee before thee seven ways" (Deuteronomy 28:7).

Expect God to bless you for every act of obedience. "And it shall come to pass, if thou shalt hearken diligently unto the voice of the Lord thy God, to observe and to do all His commandments which I command thee this day, that the Lord thy God will set thee on high above all nations of the earth: And all these blessings shall come on thee, and overtake thee, if thou shalt hearken unto the voice of the Lord thy God" (Deuteronomy 28:1, 2).

A businessman approached me. "I don't really believe Jesus really meant what He said about the hundredfold. We've misunderstood that."

"So, you intend to teach Jesus how to talk when you get to heaven?" I laughed.

If He will do it for a papaya...He will do it for you and me. We are His children, not merely fruit on a tree!

I believe one of the major reasons people do not experience a supernatural abundant Harvest in finances is because they really do not expect Jesus to do what He said He would do.

Low expectations affect God.

When you sow with expectation your "Seed" will stand before God as a testimony of your faith and confidences.

▶ Sow, expecting God to respond favorably to every act of confidence in Him.

▶ Sow, from every paycheck.

▶ Sow, *expectantly, generously and faithfully.*

When you start looking and expecting God to fulfill His promise the Harvest you've needed so long will come more quickly and bountiful than you've ever dreamed.

Let's pray:

"Father, teach us the Wonder of Expectation. Show us how it pleasures You to be believed. Hasten the Harvest as we depend on Your incredible integrity. In Jesus' name. Amen."

～ 17 ～

Many Do Not Pursue A Harvest, Because They Have Not Yet Tasted The Pain Of Poverty.

Poverty Is A Tormentor.

Poverty is wrenching, tormenting, devastating and heartbreaking.

Poverty is the climate where the Seeds of suicide grow and flourish. It strips a man of his self-confidence and sense of worth. It blurs the visions of his dreams and goals. Focus is broken.

Poverty is where the weeds of anger and cynicism grow the quickest. I cannot think of anything good about poverty.

Yet, many have not learned to despise the chains of bankruptcy and poverty.

Poverty is *not a friend* with whom to negotiate.

Poverty is an *enemy to be destroyed.*

Poverty is captivity. It's slavery. You must recognize that financial *captivity* is unnatural. You must develop a hatred to smash the chains that hold you back from financial abundance.

You may never taste the financial success you

deserve until you see the tragedy of loss, bankruptcy and poverty. I have walked the streets of Calcutta, India, and watched children with fingers inside of food cans trying to find some moist soup or something left in a can so they can survive. I have watched wagons roll through the streets of Calcutta picking up the dead bodies of people who died along the sidewalks at night. Yes, I have watched them burn those bodies and people weeping and crying... *because of poverty.*

Poverty stops us from building more great churches, uncommon television ministries, and radio evangelism. It stops a missionary from having enough to start another ten thousand churches for God.

Poverty is a spirit. It happens *inside* you before it happens *around* you. Men deteriorate inwardly before their business deteriorates.

Jesus knew an enemy existed. "The thief cometh not, but for to steal, and to kill, and to destroy: I am come that they might have life, and that they might have it more abundantly" (John 10:10).

Poverty produces fear. Fear of failure. Fear that others will not respect us and treat us properly.

Poverty produces insecurity and suspicion toward every other person around you.

How do I know that poverty is a "spirit?" It crushes and destroys the spirit of man that should be alive, vibrant and victorious. Poverty makes you want to quit instead of succeed.

The spirit of poverty will make you critical of those who are trying to set you free from it.

I will never forget the service in Houston, Texas, as long as I live. When I finished teaching, I shared for a few moments about *aiming your Seed like an arrow.* An anointing came upon me in a powerful and unusual way. I asked the people to prepare a special Seed to plant into the work of God.

Suddenly, like a volcano, a man sitting on the second row jumped to his feet yelling. He rushed to the aisle and raced to the back of the church shouting. Just as he reached the front door of the church to leave, I called out to him to stop. I asked him to state clearly what was bothering him.

He was almost crying with a mixture of rage, shame and question. "What do you tell your 13 year old daughter when she asks you for a dollar and you don't even have enough to give to her?" he shouted. "I have been out of work for two years. I have no money. When my teenage daughter asked for an offering to give a few moments ago, I had nothing!"

"That's the reason I am teaching these principles to you, my precious brother." I explained gently. My heart went out to him.

Oh, *poverty is a cruel task master.*

> **Poverty Is A Spirit That Rebels Most In The Presence Of A Deliverer Who Can Cast it Out.**

Poverty will make you doubt every good thing about yourself.

Poverty will make you question the truth about God, your true Source and Provider. It will make you hate every minister who teaches on prosperity. This is one of the proofs that poverty is a spirit — it *reacts the strongest to the person who can cast it out.*

Poverty is not merely a financial circumstance in your life. Poverty is a spiritual condition of your heart and soul.

Poverty destroys normality. You draw unwise and ridiculous conclusions. You make wrong decisions. Poverty generally multiplies to those who are poor. *It takes an incredible impact and revelation to destroy the spirit of poverty in your life.*

Let me explain. My teaching on the supernatural provision of God should have excited my brother. He should have leaped on his feet with joy! He should have cried out, "Yes! I despise poverty. Thank you for coming to set me free."

This did not happen. He was angry. He was ashamed. *The message was intimidating to him.* Why? The spirit of poverty had its claws so deeply imbedded into him, he needed a supernatural experience with a divine Deliverer, the Holy Spirit.

"The Spirit of the Lord God is upon me; because the Lord hath anointed me to preach good tidings unto the meek; He hath sent me to bind up the brokenhearted, to proclaim liberty to the captives, and the opening of the prison to them that are bound" (Isaiah 61:1).

Jesus is our Deliverer. "If the Son therefore shall make you free, ye shall be free indeed" (John 8:36).

I looked with great compassion at my poor broken brother.

"Come back here, my brother." He didn't really want to go back to his seat, but the anointing was so strong on me, he had to obey.

"My brother, this is the very reason that we are sowing Seed today — to break the spirit of poverty on the body of Christ and people who have been broken and bruised."

Normally, I would have carried the offering back

to our offices in Dallas where it would be deposited in the ministry account. Then, we would purchase television and radio air time, pay our employees, and purchase books and so forth with the finances. But, an unusual anointing covered me like a magnificent mantle. I announced to the entire church a new instruction.

"I want to sow this entire offering into my brother and his family who have been without a job for two years. This Seed will grow for every person who plants it. Because the Bible says, 'He that hath pity upon the poor lendeth unto the Lord; and that which he hath given will He pay him again'" (Proverbs 19:17). The people clapped their hands with joy. The man was embarrassed at first. I reassured him that this was the leading of the Holy Spirit. God was using this offering to remind him of His deep love and commitment to him and his family.

Fear Makes You Hoard. Hoarding Stops The Flow Of Increase So The Poor Stay In The Cycle Of Poverty.

His poverty had birthed fear. Fear Makes You *Hoard.* Hoarding Stops The Flow Of Increase. Consequently, those who are poor usually get in a debt cycle that is never broken.

Poverty brings fear. The fear causes them to hoard and hold back their finances. Hoarding is the opposite of giving. So hoarding cuts off any connection to the supply. *The death cycle of the poor never seems to stop.*

It takes an anointing, an uncommon anointing, for financial blessing. "And it shall come to pass in that day, that his burden shall be taken away from off thy shoulder, and his yoke from off thy neck, and the yoke shall be destroyed because of the anointing" (Isaiah 10:27).

The anointing on a servant of God can break the back of poverty in a person's life. Since God is the Provider, the Multiplier and the Source of supply, He wants His people to be financially prosperous. Perhaps, this is one of the reasons He warns us to keep our hands off His leaders. "Saying, Touch not Mine anointed, and do My prophets no harm" (Psalm 105:15).

A businessman wished to enter into a small debate over the issue. I was visiting his home. He was anti-prosperity, anti-preachers, and anti-everything.

I interrogated him lightly. His father had given him his money from his business. His father owned his home. He was the son of a wealthy man. He had little appreciation for the toil, labor and time involved in generating a financially successful life.

He was a parasite who had never faced poverty as an enemy. That's why he was not pursuing a Harvest. He was living off of others instead.

Many years ago, thousands of hippies throughout our colleges sneered at money, achievement and productivity. Where did they find the time and energy to criticize? Their parents were paying their college bills, sending them checks for spending money, and making their car payments. *They were not tasting the pain of poverty.*

When you stare woodenly at a stack of bills that is impossible to pay, only then will gratitude and thankfulness begin to flow in your life for the supernatural Harvest.

When your children are sick and finances prevent you from purchasing adequate care, *you will taste the pain of poverty.*

When you watch movers take the furniture out of your house and load it in a truck to go back to the store where it was purchased, *you will taste the pain of poverty.*

When you are threatened with a lawsuit, and have not a cent in your account to defend yourself, *you will understand the pain of poverty.*

When you look through your dresser drawers to find coins to buy a loaf of bread because you have been out of work three months, *you will understand the pain of poverty.*

When you truly understand the sorrow poverty and the tragedy of lack, your faith will begin to focus on the laws of provision, the financial Harvest God guaranteed.

Thousands have not yet hit the bottom. Someone keeps cushioning their fall. A mother slips some money to her lazy son. A father, guilty for not spending more time with his son, buys him a new car. Consequently, they never really taste the emptiness of poverty.

That's one of the reasons some will never walk in a supernatural supply. Their needs are never really big enough to force them to pursue a Harvest.

Let's pray:

"Father, don't let me have to taste the pain of poverty before I appreciate Your blessing. I need your anointing to break the spirit of poverty in my life. You are my Deliverer and I celebrate the Promise of Plenty You have made to me. In Jesus' name. Amen."

∽ Leviticus 27:30 ∽

"And all the tithe of the land, whether of the
seed of the land, or of the fruit of the tree, is
the Lord's: it is holy unto the Lord."

❧ 18 ❧

MILLIONS STEAL THE TITHE, THE HOLY PORTION GOD RESERVED FOR HIMSELF.

When You Keep The Tithe, You Commit Theft.

When you take something that belongs to another, you are a thief. Thieves will not enter heaven. "But lay up for yourselves treasures in heaven, where neither moth nor rust doth corrupt, and where thieves do not break through nor steal:" (Matthew 6:20).

Tithe means "tenth." The great patriarch, and wonderful example, Abraham, gave ten percent of his income back as proof and evidence that he honored God as his Provider and was blessed incredibly for it. "And Abram was very rich in cattle, in silver, and in gold" (Genesis 13:2).

Isaac, his son, continued to reap from the life of obedience. "Then Isaac sowed in that land, and received in the same year an hundredfold: and the Lord blessed him. And the man waxed great, and went forward, and grew until he became very great: For he had possession of flocks, and possession of herds, and great store of servants: and the Philistines envied him" (Genesis 26:12-14).

It happened for the children of Abraham. "And

> **When You Tithe, You Create A Financial Flow For Several Generations After You.**

the Lord appeared unto him the same night, and said, I am the God of Abraham thy father: fear not, for I am with thee, and will bless thee, and multiply thy Seed *for My servant Abraham's sake*" (Genesis 26:24).

The tithe is holy unto the Lord. "And all the tithe of the land, whether of the Seed of the land, or of the fruit of the tree, is the Lord's: it is holy unto the Lord" (Leviticus 27:30).

Your tithe is the Golden Gate to financial supply. "Bring ye all the tithes into the storehouse, that there may be meat in Mine house, and prove Me now herewith, saith the Lord of hosts, if I will not open you the windows of heaven, and pour you out a blessing, that there shall not be room enough to receive it" (Malachi 3:10).

The arrogant will not tithe. You see, there are three kinds of atheists: 1) those who believe that God does not even exist; 2) those who believe they are capable of doing anything God could do; and 3) those who consider themselves as god in their own life. A non-tither's position is like the atheist — they keep the tithe. They feel that they are their own god in their own life. It is the ultimate proof of arrogance and pride.

Honor the tithe. Tithing is the Biblical practice of returning ten percent of your income back to God *after* you have earned it. In the Old Testament, Abraham and others tithed. In the New Testament, even the Pharisees, the hypocritical religious crowd, remembered to tithe. "This *ought* to have done...."

"And concerning the tithe of the herd, or of the flock, even of whatsoever passeth under the rod, the tenth shall be holy unto the Lord" (Leviticus 27:32).

Tithing can break the financial curse on your life and family. You see, those who rob God of the tithe and offerings that belong to Him are living under a curse.

Oh my friend, you can change this. You can be the member of your family that "breaks the curse." Your Seed is the proof of your faith. It is the proof that you have conquered greed. Obviously, God always penalizes a thief. But, He always promotes and prospers the tither and those who sow Seed. "Will a man rob God? Yet ye have robbed Me. But ye say, Wherein have we robbed Thee? In tithes and offerings. Ye are cursed with a curse: for ye have robbed Me, even this whole nation" (Malachi 3:8).

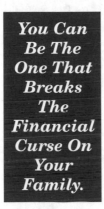

You Can Be The One That Breaks The Financial Curse On Your Family.

Tithe consistently. Each tithe is an act of faith, a Seed of obedience that creates momentum. When you tithe consistently, you will create a consistent Harvest. Establish a rhythm. *Stay in obedience long enough to taste the rewards of momentum.*

There are four basic seasons each year. Regularity and routine are very important forces in our lives, especially in a Seed-faith lifestyle. Work with the law of sowing and reaping. Don't become erratic and unpredictable. Nature itself has a pattern, a rhythm and routine. When you honor it, the benefits will far outweigh any cost and risk involved. "While the earth remaineth, Seedtime and Harvest, and cold and heat, and summer and winter, and day and night shall not cease" (Genesis 8:22).

Tithing is the proof you have conquered greed.

Satan steals. Man hoards. God gives. *Your giving is the only proof that God lives within you.* It is the only evidence that the nature of God is flourishing inside your heart. Whether it is money, mercy or love, *giving is the only real evidence of love.* "For God so loved the world, that He gave..." (John 3:16).

When you tithe, you create a memory in the mind of God forever. He beholds His nature in you.

"For God hath not given us the spirit of fear; but of power, and of love, and of a sound mind" (2 Timothy 1:7). Fear torments. It makes you hoard instead of release. You become afraid that you can never replace the money that you are "giving to God." The truth? The tithe is already His. *He permits you the privilege of returning it to Him as proof of your confidence in Him.*

Tithing is the proof that you believe the Word of God to you. The Word of God is a collection of instructions. God wants so much to be believed. He

Tithing Is The Proof You Have Mastered Fear.

promised that those who would tithe and bring offerings to Him would see a financial Harvest as a result. "But he shall receive an hundredfold now in this time, houses, and brethren, and sisters, and mothers, and children, and lands, with perse-cutions; and in the world to come eternal life" (Mark 10:30).

The Old Testament confirms it. "Honour the Lord with thy substance, and with the firstfruits of all thine increase: So shall thy barns be filled with plenty, and thy presses shall burst out with new wine" (Proverbs 3:9, 10).

When you write out a check for ten percent of your income each week and give it back to God, it documents your faith in God. It is proof of your confidence. You really do believe that His Word works. You have fully embraced the wonderful truth that "God is not a man, that He should lie; neither the son of man, that He should repent: hath He said, and shall He not do it? or hath He spoken, and shall He not make it good?" (Numbers 23:19).

Yet, millions attend church every Sunday and walk out with the holy tithe still in their pockets. Sometimes, they will drop a few dollars in its place in the offering as a substitution.

Picture something with me for a few moments. Suppose a businessman flew home from a business transaction. His son meets him at the airport. The father excited, puts his arm around his son and says, "I really love you son. I'm so proud of you. Here's a $10 bill to buy yourself a little present. I just made $100 extra that I had not planned on in this business deal."

"Thanks, dad!"

"Well, son, go ahead and take several more of these $10 bills. Actually, you can have nine of these $10 bills for yourself. I will just keep one with me for some change," the father remarks, good naturedly.

Think further with me. Both go home. The son goes into his bedroom to sleep that night. The father takes everything out of his pockets, leaving the tenth $10 bill inside the dresser drawer. He goes to sleep.

During the night, the son cannot sleep. He turns and tosses. He is thankful for the nine $10 bills ($90) that his father gave him. But, something inside him that he cannot explain makes him keep thinking about that $10 bill in his father's dresser drawer. What if the son sneaked up in the middle of the night, opened the dresser drawer and took and stole the tenth $10 bill? What are your feelings about that? I imagine you would be incensed and infuriated. You would exclaim with anger, "That son is an idiot, a fool and a thief. He was so unthankful for the $90 that his father gave him, he stole the tenth."

Yet, this happens every single Sunday on earth. Somehow, our ingratitude and unthankfulness begins to choke out every word of praise that should be flowing from our lips. Instead of gratitude and thankfulness for our health, our energy, favor, and friendships — the last $10 bill is stolen...from the hand of the very One who gave the other $90 to us.

Another scenario. Just suppose that I told you that the son left a $1 bill in its place in his father's drawer — thinking his father would not notice the difference between a $1 bill and the $10 bill. Maybe, he feels that his father would not notice the missing zero!

This would be a substitution.

He steals the $10 by replacing it with a $1 bill.

Yes, you are angry again. Yet, this too happens in every church in America every single Sunday morning. Thousands substitute a small offering in place of the tithe. Do we think God is that stupid?

I held six seminars for six consecutive Friday evenings in Austin, Texas. The young man who shined my shoes in the Austin airport was so impressive. I loved him, his little wife and child. One day, he spoke to me. "Mike, I love my pastor. The music in our church is just fantastic. However, there is one thing that I despise and makes me so angry every Sunday. Every time I attend my church, my pastor wants to talk about offerings. It seems to me that's all he talks about — tithe and offerings, tithe and offerings, tithe and offerings."

"Has anyone ever explained the tithe to you?" I

asked.

He could not remember having anyone explain it to him. So, I proceeded to explain that *everything* we have *came from God.*

God established a system that would destroy the possibility of greed, the tithe. God is not poor. Angels are not on ration. Mansions in heaven are not half finished. God said that everything already belonged to Him anyway. But, He established a system that

God Established A System That Would Destroy The Possibility Of Greed, The Tithe.

would permit man to *destroy his greatest enemy of prosperity, greed.* It was simple. Bring ten percent back to God, and He promised to bless you again and again for such obedience.

Then, I explained that God guaranteed a curse on anyone who stole the holy part (Malachi 3:9-11). The words of Jesus were also explained carefully. When Peter felt that he had lost everything in order to follow after Jesus, Jesus reminded him of a wonderful result...the one hundredfold return principle (Mark 10:28-30).

My young shoe shine friend was ecstatic. He had never understood the Law of the Hundredfold Return.

It is not a mystery. It happens everyday everywhere around us. A farmer once told me about the Law of Return in a kernel of corn.

"Mike, one kernel of corn can produce a cornstalk. Each cornstalk produces four corncobs. Some have counted as high as 700 kernels of corn on a single corncob, meaning that one kernel of corn can produce 2,800 more kernels of corn on those four different corncobs combined. So, a hundredfold return is not at all a miracle. It is a normal fact of life in the Law of Return."

The young man agreed to do something I asked.

"I want you to tithe every Sunday morning at your church." The Bible says, "Upon the first day of the week let every one of you lay by him in store, as God has prospered him" (1 Corinthians 16:2).

I continued. "Tithe habitually, without interruption, for four seasons, the next 12 months. You see, if you have been sowing Seeds of Nothing, you have already *scheduled* 'Seasons of Nothing' in your future. A Seed reproduces itself. So, if you have been bringing nothing to God, you have been scheduling Seasons of Nothing in your future. Give God a chance to cycle you through the Seasons of Nothing until you can begin to see a Harvest in your life," I explained.

Tithing Destroys Greed, The Greatest Enemy Prosperity Has Ever Known.

He agreed.

God did it quicker than I ever imagined. In less than 30 days, he stood in a small prayer breakfast I held at the Hilton Hotel in Austin, Texas, shouting, "It works!"

His tip money for the first seven days after his commitment to tithe was over $800. He had never experienced this kind of income in his life. Today, someone told me he had started a small chain of shoe shine places, and people are working for him!

Millions will never taste the financial Harvest that's within their reach because they have stolen the holy tithe and kept it for themselves. The ultimate act of arrogance.

⮞ 19 ⮜

Many Refuse To Sow During Times Of Crisis.

Crisis Creates Fear.

It happened to me several years ago. Through a parade of tragedies, personal and in my ministry, I suddenly faced bankruptcy. I owed many times more than what I owned. I did not know what to do. I prayed, fasted, and used every business principle I knew. The wall refused to budge. It was like a mountain of debt that nothing could shake.

I became intimidated. I felt like a failure. Other ministries were flourishing and were building huge buildings. I couldn't even pay my CPA $1,500 to get a financial statement to present to the bank *for a loan!* I met with successful businessmen who offered to loan me $250,000...if I would pay them $50,000 immediately. (I did not have $5,000 cash to my name!)

During those times, satan really appeared overpowering. Sometimes it's hard to truly believe that your pain will ever pass.

I couldn't think straight. I would sit numbly in various meetings around the table of negotiation.

My mind was in shock. My heart lost its fight. I could not budge the wall of debt. (Sometimes, during the battles of life, you will be tempted to withdraw, become timid and passive.) You see, satan is a bully. Bullies delight in shy, timid peace makers.

It is important that you develop a fighting spirit. Very important. "Resist the devil, and he will flee from you" (James 4:7).

You must run toward your Goliath. David did. But, he did not come in his own strength against his enemy. He came "in the name of the Lord."

Crisis is the place of miracles. It is not the place to shrink back, quit and hoard your sowing. I was so tempted to stop giving. I felt that the ministry needed to "keep the tithe for itself." Crisis distorts every *picture of prosperity.*

Why is crisis time an important season to sow?

1) *Your sowing will birth expectation and hope.*

2) *Expectation is the only magnet that attracts the miracle provision God promised.* "Without faith it is impossible to please Him: for he that cometh to God must believe that He is, and that He is a rewarder of them that diligently seek Him" (Hebrews 11:6).

3) *If you refuse to sow, you have just destroyed your own ability to expect a miracle.* A farmer can only expect a Harvest after he has planted Seed.

▶ So, *your sowing is what births* your expectation.

▶ Your expectation is the current that brings the one hundredfold return Jesus promised.

4) *Nothing is going to change for you financially until you can unleash expectation within you.*

5) *Your crisis actually magnifies the size of your Seed in the eyes of God.* Your Seed will increase in its influence with God...*because of your crisis situation.* Jesus was watching the offering one day. He "beheld how the people cast money into the treasury: and many that were rich cast in much. And there came a certain poor widow, she threw in two mites, which make a farthing."

> **Your Crisis Increases The Influence Of Your Seed With God.**

This contained a powerful insight. He shared with His disciples. "This poor widow hath cast more in than all they which hath cast into the treasury: For all they did cast in of their abundance; but she of her want did cast in all that she had, even all her living" (Mark 12:41-44). She did not have very much money. She was poor. But, her financial crisis *enlarged her Seed* in the eyes of God. She gave more than everyone else, in His opinion, because of her crisis.

That's why it is important to plant Seed when your back is against the wall, and you have very little. *Your Seed will carry more weight, influence and potential for increase than a much larger Seed will have later when you are doing quite well.*

Thousands hoard during crisis.

It is the most unwise thing they could ever do.

If you will sow during times of famine, your Seed will move the heavens and open the windows. God will pour you out a blessing you can hardly contain.

≈ Lamentations 3:25 ≈

"The Lord is good unto them that wait for
him, to the soul that seeketh him."

———⊳●⊲———

~ 20 ~

SOME REFUSE TO WAIT LONG ENOUGH FOR THEIR HARVEST.

Time Is The Hidden And Mysterious Ingredient In An Uncommon Harvest.

You see, Patience is a Seed, too. "The Lord is good unto them that wait for Him, to the soul that seeketh Him" (Lamentations 3:25).

Waiting Is The Forgotten But Powerful Season Between Sowing And Reaping.

Your waiting reveals trust. "It is good that man should both hope and quietly wait for the salvation of the Lord" (Lamentations 3:26).

Your waiting may be painful. But, it is the season between sowing and reaping. That's why the Bible calls it — Seedtime, and Harvest. *Time is the season between the Seed and the Harvest.* "Weeping may endure for a night, but joy cometh in the morning" (Psalm 30:5).

Some of you have lost your Harvest because of the pain of waiting. Waiting is burdensome. It breeds agitation, a critical spirit and can leave you frustrated.

While waiting, words of doubt and unbelief are

spoken. This often aborts the *cycle of blessing*. Unthankfulness brings a curse, not a reward. Ingratitude does not inspire God to hasten the Harvest.

It stops the Harvest.

You must be willing to trust God through the seasons of waiting. He has promised a change.

Your *anger* does not intimidate God.

Your *schedule* does not obligate God.

He is God. He will decide when you deserve and qualify for the Harvest. "For My thoughts are not your thoughts, neither are your ways My ways, saith the Lord. For as the heavens are higher than the earth, so are My ways higher than your ways, and My thoughts than your thoughts" (Isaiah 55:8, 9).

He has already promised your Harvest in due season. "For as the rain cometh down, and the snow from heaven, and returneth not thither, but watereth the earth, and maketh it bring forth and bud that it may give Seed to the sower, and bread to the eater: so shall My Word be that goeth forth out of My mouth: it shall not return unto Me void, but it shall accomplish that which I please, and it shall prosper in the thing whereto I sent it" (Isaiah 55:10, 11).

Get excited about your Harvest. "For ye shall go out with joy, and be led forth with peace: the mountains and the hills shall break forth before you into singing, and all the trees of the field shall clap their hands" (Isaiah 55:12).

God will replace every financial disaster with a financial miracle. "Instead of the thorn shall come up the fir tree, and instead of the brier shall come up the myrtle tree: and it shall be to the Lord for a name, for an everlasting sign that shall not be cut off" (Isaiah 55:13).

You must refuse to permit words of discouragement in your mouth. "Fear thou not; for I am with thee: be not dismayed; for I am thy God: I will strengthen thee; yea, I will help thee; yea, I will uphold thee with the right hand of My righteousness" (Isaiah 41:10).

Those who oppose and battle against your progress, will be confronted by God Himself. "Behold, all they that were incensed against thee shall be ashamed and confounded: they shall be as nothing; and they that strive with thee shall perish" (Isaiah 41:11).

Your enemies shall not succeed against you. "Thou shalt seek them, and shall not find them, even them that contended with thee: they that war against thee shall be as nothing, and as a thing of nought. For I the Lord thy God will hold thy right hand, saying unto thee, Fear not; I will help thee" (Isaiah 41:12-13).

The Holy Spirit is involved against your enemy. "When the enemy shall come in like a flood, the Spirit of the Lord shall lift up a standard against him" (Isaiah 59:19).

Every scheme, strategy and trap against you shall ultimately fail if you will be patient in waiting. "No weapon that is formed against thee shall prosper; and every tongue that shall rise against thee in judgment thou shalt condemn. This is the heritage of the servants of the Lord, and their righteousness is of me, saith the Lord" (Isaiah 54:17).

Keep your eyes upon the rewards that will follow your waiting. Men fight for a reason — to gain something they want. When David faced Goliath, he was fully aware of the benefits offered to the person who could defeat Goliath. He would have the hand of the king's daughter. He would not have to pay any taxes. So, armed with the inner picture of his success and its rewards, he ran to Goliath to conquer him.

Jesus went to Calvary, fully aware of the resurrection — "for the joy that was set before Him."

Keep focused. The spoils of war are worth the battle and the tormenting season called waiting.

Refuse to sin with your mouth. Your enemy reacts to your words. If you feed on doubt and unbelief, it will energize and motivate him to rise up against you.

Never speak words that encourage your enemy. Your enemy will believe anything you are telling him. If you feed faith words into his ear, he will be demoralized, disappointed and discouraged. If you talk like a *victim,* he'll be encouraged to attack you again and again and again. "Death and life are in the power of the tongue: and they that love it shall eat the fruit thereof" (Proverbs 18:21).

Your words of faith will always influence the heart of God. "For by thy words thou shalt be justified, and by thy words thou shalt be condemned" (Matthew 12:37).

While you are waiting, create a climate of gratitude and thanksgiving. "In every thing give thanks: for this is the will of God in Christ Jesus concerning you" (1 Thessalonians 5:18).

Continuously pray in the Spirit throughout the day. "Pray without ceasing" (1 Thessalonians 5:17). "But ye, beloved, building up yourselves on your most holy faith, praying in the Holy Ghost" (Jude 20).

Avoid the temptation to create a backup plan. "Neither give place to the devil" (Ephesians 4:27).

When one of the great explorers came to America, he burned the ships behind him and his soldiers. It made escape impossible. It made exploration a necessity and requirement. His men could not go back. *You cannot plan your success and failure at the same time.* Your success will require your total focus and attention.

Make no plans to go backwards.

Fuel, energize and strengthen the picture of your future. This develops your faith. Discuss with everyone the miracle that is en route to you. Work on your expectation. Obedience is always rewarded. Everything God has promised you will come to pass. "All these blessings shall come on thee, and overtake thee, if thou shalt hearken unto the voice of the Lord thy God" (Deuteronomy 28:2). Your life lived holy produces results. "No good thing will He withhold from them that walk uprightly" (Psalm 84:11).

You are not fighting your battle alone. "I will be an enemy unto thine enemies, and an adversary unto thine adversaries" (Exodus 23:22).

Refuse to give anyone access to yourself who is not in agreement with the Word of God. When satan wants to destroy you, he sends a person into your life. "Be not deceived: evil communications corrupt good manners" (1 Corinthians 15:33).

Avoid broken focus. *When the wrong people talk to you, you make the wrong decisions.*

When you make a mistake, consider yourself that much closer to your Harvest. "The Lord upholdeth all that fall, and raiseth up all those that be bowed down" (Psalm 145:14). Don't be too hard on yourself.

The rewards of change are coming. Patience works. *Overcoming involves more than one battle.* It is the man who refuses to quit that wins. Always.

Never consider quitting. Never. Get up and try again. And, again. And, again. Hell fears a fighter. "Blessed is the man that endureth temptation: for when he is tried, he shall receive the crown of life, which the Lord hath promised to them that love Him" (James 1:12).

My greatest blessings have come after my longest waiting.

Several years ago, I was preaching for Rod Parsley, a friend of mine, in Columbus, Ohio. At the end of the service, the Holy Spirit spoke to me to receive an offering for the pastor instead of my own ministry. Well, I desperately needed a miracle. I needed finances badly for a special project I was facing. So, any Seed I planted would be a Crisis Seed. (Remember that a Crisis Seed increases in its influence with God.) *It is possible that a small Seed sown during a crisis produces a greater Harvest than a generous Seed during good times.*

So, I agreed to give the offering in its entirety to the pastor. Then, the Holy Spirit made an unusual suggestion. I really did not feel that it was a command but rather an *invitation to an investment.* I had just received a royalty check for $8,500. (Actually, it was everything that I had to my name.) I do not recall any money in my savings account other than this check I had in my briefcase.

"How would you like to explore and experiment what I could do with your $8,500?" the Holy Spirit spoke.

It brought a moment of torment and torture.

Then, I just quietly spoke in my spirit back to Him, "That's all right. I really appreciate this wonderful $8,500! It is enough Harvest for me."

He spoke the second time. Oh, how thankful I am for the *second chances* He gives to us to try again, reach again, and plant again.

"How would you like to explore and experiment with what I could do with your $8,500?"

Something in me took a careful evaluation. What could I really do with $8,500? It certainly was not enough to pay my house off. What could I do? Buy a small car, or put a down payment on a rent house, or fly to Europe and vacation for a month?

I decided to believe His Word.

That decision changed my lifetime income forever.

Six weeks later, God gave me an idea that brought me hundreds of thousands of dollars in return. In fact, every 90 days I receive a royalty check for that idea.

Now, here is the powerful principle about waiting that you must grasp.

It was over two years after I sowed the $8,500 that I received my first nickel of profit from that idea. I went through several battles and difficulties. I thought the idea would never get off the ground. But, it did. My willingness to wait through eight seasons of Harvest was worth every single hour of waiting.

Some want to plant on Sunday morning in church and reap Monday morning on their job. That is not even logical, Scriptural, or promised by God. "But he that endureth to the end shall be saved" (Matthew 10:22).

Keep feeding your faith during the painful

season of waiting. "So then faith cometh by hearing and hearing by the word of God" (Romans 10:17).

Your seasons of waiting are not seasons of inactivity. Much is going on. Angels are positioning to minister. Demons are being confronted. Strategies are being developed. God is moving people into your life just like a Boaz was moved into the life of Ruth. Never believe that a season of waiting is a season of doing nothing. *The opposite is true.*

Seasons of waiting are the busiest seasons ever in the Spirit world.

Remind yourself that joy still flows in the heat of battle. "And you became followers of us, and of the Lord, having received the Word in much affliction, with joy of the Holy Ghost" (1 Thessalonians 1:6).

Do not permit your Ship of Financial Harvest to be dashed on the Rock of Impatience. Thousands have not received their financial Harvest because they got in a hurry, unwilling to trust the Lord of the Harvest for His timing. "But they that wait upon the Lord shall renew their strength; they shall mount up with wings as eagles; they shall run, and not be weary; and they shall walk, and not faint" (Isaiah 40:31).

Let's pray:

"Father, you do all things well. You understand the Seasons. I don't Give me the ability to wait. Your timing is perfect. Your schedule is better than mine. I will trust You, wait on You, and You will reward me abundantly. In Jesus' name. Amen."

≈ 21 ≈

Millions Refuse To Obey The Very Basic And Simple Laws Of God.

Disobedience Produces Losses.

The Scriptures warn. "If ye be willing and obedient, ye shall eat the good of the land: but if ye refuse and rebel ye shall be devoured with the sword: for the mouth of the Lord hath spoken it" (Isaiah 1:19, 20).

You can argue about it.

You can rebel against it.

You can complain about it.

But, you cannot read the Scriptures without understanding clearly that obedience produces the river of blessing while *disobedience brings famine* and desolation.

"Oh, I know some wealthy people who do not serve God at all. They do not attend church, and they do not read the Scriptures. So, why are they prospering?" Good question. And, quite easy to answer, too.

They are probably obeying the *basic principles* of prosperity established in Scripture.

Let's look at some of these principles and laws

that are established quite clearly in Scripture. God said, "And it shall come to pass, if thou shalt hearken diligently unto the voice of the Lord thy God, to observe and to do all His commandments which I command thee this day, that the Lord thy God will set thee on high above all nations of the earth: and all these blessings shall come on thee, and overtake thee, if thou shalt hearken unto the voice of the Lord thy God" (Deuteronomy 28:1, 2).

1. *The Principle of Work.* God only promised to bless the work of your hands. "The Lord shall open unto thee His good treasure, the heaven to give the rain unto thy land in His season, and to bless all the work of thine hand" (Deuteronomy 28:12). It is not an option. It is not merely a good "idea" to work every day. The Apostle Paul wrote that those who refuse to be productive *should be denied food.* "For even when we were with you, this we commanded you, that if any would not work, neither should he eat" (2 Thessalonians 3:10).

Those who refuse to work are called disorderly and busybodies in other people's business. "For we hear that there are some which walk among you disorderly, *working not at all*, but are busybodies" (2 Thessalonians 3:11).

You must withdraw and withhold any friendship and time of fellowship with those rebellious toward working. "And if any man obey not our word by this epistle, note that man, and have no company with him, that he may be ashamed" (2 Thessalonians 3:14). *Note that man.* In other words, draw attention to that man. Everyone should mark the lazy person.

"But, I lost my good job. I am waiting for one better to come along," one girl complained.

The principle of work simply reveals the need to be productive. Joseph was productive. He was not in the perfect place, the prison, when he received his promotion. But, he produced and solved problems *wherever God placed him.* As I told a young man working for me one day, "Son, you may not enjoy what you are doing here in this ministry right now. But, if you don't become productive and complete the instructions I am already giving you, the next season will not be a step up. God will make you run the same lap over and over and over again until you learn this principle."

2. *The Principle of Diligence.* Diligence means speedy attention to an assigned task. "He becometh poor that dealeth with a slack hand: but the hand of the diligent maketh rich" (Proverbs 10:4). Laziness is one of the many reasons people do not experience financial Harvest. "But he that sleepeth in Harvest is a son that causeth shame" (Proverbs 10:5).

Diligent people become supervisors and leaders. "The hand of the diligent shall bear rule" (Proverbs 12:24).

The diligent will always have plenty. "The soul of the sluggard desireth, and hath nothing: but the soul of the diligent shall be made fat" (Proverbs 13:4).

Those who are diligent become creative in discovering new ways to solve problems. "The thoughts of the diligent tend only to plenteousness..." (Proverbs 21:5).

Leaders pursue the company and presence of diligent workers. "Seest thou a man diligent in his business? He shall stand before kings" (Proverbs 22:29).

The diligent continuously evaluate the results of their efforts. "Be thou diligent to know the state of thy flocks, and look well to thy herds" (Proverbs 27:23).

Find the problem closest to you and solve it.

Ask others how to bear the burdens they are presently bearing. Listen carefully to things that bring strife to your boss. Solve them.

▶ Review your master list of tasks and complete them one by one every single day.

▶ Labor for *completions* instead of allowing a project to run on and on.

▶ Pursue correction from the one who signs your paycheck.

▶ Accept rebuke with *thankfulness* instead of retaliation and resentment.

▶ Flourish where you are presently working and the news will travel.

3. *The Principle of Wisdom.* When you increase Wisdom, you will increase your wealth. "Counsel is Mine, and sound Wisdom... riches and honour are with Me; yea, durable riches and righteousness... that I may cause those that love Me to inherit substance; and I will fill their treasures" (Proverbs 8:14-21).

You must become good at what you do.

Study, attend seminars and be mentored. "Wise men lay up knowledge" (Proverbs 10:14).

Rich people are usually knowledgeable people. "Happy is the man that findeth Wisdom... length of days is in her right hand; and in her left hand riches and honour" (Proverbs 3:13, 16). They may not know everything about everything — but they are skilled and develop in at least one topic of their chosen pursuit. You must find the gifts and skills already planted within you.

What you love is a clue to the Wisdom you

contain. If you love computers, that is a clue that you will have special Wisdom in that area. If you have a love for children, you will have a Wisdom toward children.

▶ When you find what you love, you will find your Wisdom.

▶ When you find your Wisdom, you will be paid to solve problems with it.

4. *The Principle of Waiting.* Nobody wants to wait for anything. Sam Walton, the late billionaire, once said that he never invested in a company for where it would be within 18 months. He examined carefully to see where the company would arrive within ten years or longer. Some Japanese businessmen have 100-year goals. A friend of mine once told me that if my father had put $100 a month in a special money market account, I would have been a multimillionaire on my twentieth birthday.

"Then, why isn't everyone a millionaire if $100 a month put aside for 20 years could create such wealth?" I asked.

"Nobody wants to wait 20 years to spend their $100," was his reply.

What is the proof that people will not wait? When they receive a raise on their job, they immediately make a purchase to obligate that raise. Instead of living within the boundaries of their lower budget and placing the money in a special investment, they make a purchase that *produces a pleasure instead of a future.*

5. *The Principle of Mentorship.* You must be teachable. You must have a mentor. Your mentor must be someone qualified to impart knowledge for your life in the arena of finances. You can have a spiritual mentor who is marvelous in prayer and yet

unlearned in finances. You can have someone who wants to teach you their opinions, but who does not have any financial success to substantiate and support their teaching.

Who are you pursuing? What are the last three financial questions you have asked? To whom did you ask these questions? What have you done about their answers? What investment opportunities are you ignoring? Pursuing? Considering?

Recently, I felt impressed to get involved in a small financial opportunity. It would require hardly any time. But, I had faith in the head of the company. I shared it with several close to me. I even offered to help make the investment. Some embraced it immediately. Why? They trusted their instincts, my judgment, and the plan presented. Others never even showed up for the second meeting. Yet, they will complain in the coming years of their life how their financial life has been stressful, difficult and almost intolerable. But, they totally refused my mentorship regarding their finances.

"But, I've asked everyone to help me learn how to handle my finances," wailed one young lady.

"What do you want them to teach you?" I asked.

So, I took two or three hours and carefully walked her through her checkbook. I emphasized the importance of maintaining balance awareness — knowing at all times how much money is in your account. I emphasized to her the importance of keeping a small amount of cash with her at all times. She did neither. *If you refuse to follow the first two instructions of a mentor, do you qualify for a repeat visit?*

"How many have been to a certified financial planner within the last three years?" I asked a large audience one day. Three hands went up.

▶ *Everyone wants a miracle instead of mentorship.*

▶ *Quality mentorship is often the biggest miracle you need.*

Nobody can force you to pursue knowledge. Usually, it takes a tragedy to produce a desire for mentorship.

6. *The Principle of Integrity.* Integrity is simply doing what you say you will do for someone. Integrity is being what you tell everybody you are.

Integrity is truthfulness.

"If you will give me $40, I will process these four pieces of excess baggage through the airlines," said a skycap to me one day when I was at the airport. The excess was going to cost me over $200. He wanted a generous tip to do it. I always tip generously, but God had been dealing with me strongly about integrity, honesty, and doing everything the right way. You see, if nobody on earth is watching, the Boss of the universe is *always* still watching — "For the eyes of the Lord run to and fro throughout the whole earth, to show Himself strong in the behalf of them whose heart is perfect toward Him" (2 Chronicles 16:9).

"Why don't we just do the right thing?" I countered.

"Sir, it will cost you over $200," he was exasperated with me.

"I know. But, I would rather pay the excess now and feel my conscience at peace than to simply give you a large tip and save the excess baggage fee."

Thousands pad their expense account every week. Some add tips in their expense report that really did not exist or take place. Many will take extra time off for lunch and have someone use the punch-out clock for them. Many employees have taken pencils, pens, legal pads, notebooks and other supplies home to their children and family.

God sees it all. The Principle of Integrity will stand when every excuse falls apart.

Quality is a part of integrity. Show me any person who does poor work, and I'll show you a person without integrity. If you do a sloppy job of painting the house for somebody, put a used part in an automobile engine and charge for a new one you will eventually lose your business. Customers talk. Truth emerges. *Integrity will stand the test of time, criticism and even mistakes.*

Those who will lie will steal also.

You see, lying is simply *theft of the truth.* Truth is so important. It is the only ingredient that enables us to make quality decisions. So, if someone withholds from you important truths, they have stolen from you *the only ingredient you can have* to make a good decision. If someone lies to you, lock your cabinets, your doors and keep them away from your life. Even if they are relatives. The laws of God are too important to ignore.

Thousands will never walk the path to plenty because they have totally disregarded the integrity and infallibility of the Holy Scriptures and the Basic Principles of Prosperity.

～ 22 ～

THOUSANDS ARE UNWILLING TO START THEIR HARVEST WITH A SMALL SEED.

Acorns Can Become Oak Trees.

But, most people keep waiting for their "ship to come in" before they *begin* the sowing cycle. You must *start with what you have.*

This Principle of Beginning is Powerful. Every long journey starts with the first small step. Millionaires started with their first nickel. Great companies have humble beginnings. *You can go any where you want to go...if you are willing to take enough small steps.*

Look at Mary Kay Ash. She had just a few thousand dollars and a couple of shelves of products. But, she started her business. She focused on her future. Today, she is worth over 300 million dollars, and her business is worth two billion.

Look at McDonald's hamburger chain. From a humble beginning, it has become the most successful hamburger chain on the earth. It started with a little hamburger that became popular in a town.

If you keep holding on to the Seed you have today, it will never become a Harvest. You must be willing to start your Harvest with *whatever God has already placed in your hand.* I sat in a banquet many years ago frustrated. The speaker stirred me. I desperately wanted to plant a Seed of $1,000 into his ministry. But, I had only $10 in my pocket. "Lord, I really wish I could bless him with a $1,000 check," I whispered to the Lord.

"You have $10 in your pocket. Plant it."

"Oh, I need my $10 tonight. But, if You would give me $1,000, I promise to sow it," was my answer.

My mind started churning. How could I get more money to sow? I thought about my little office. It was in my tiny garage in Houston, Texas. That's where I studied, prayed, and also where I had a row of shelves that contained the only product I had in my ministry — one long-play album of music. Five hundred of those albums were on the shelves. That was approximately six to eight months of sales for me. Then it hit me. *"Start with what you already have."*

Little hinges can swing huge doors. I could give him those 500 albums. If he sold them for $6.00 each, he would make $3,000 for his ministry. I made the decision. "Brother, I wish I had a lot to give you. I wanted to be able to write a check for $1,000, but my ministry is just beginning. I do have 500 record albums. If you would receive them from me, you can sell them in your crusades. If you sell them for $1.00 each, it would be a $500 Seed. If you sell them for $6.00, you would have $3,000 for your ministry." (I thought I had to explain this to him!)

Twelve months passed. One day, while sitting in Nairobi, Kenya, at a missionary's home, the mail came. It contained a scribbled hand-written note from a major television minister. "Mike, I heard your record album. I want to purchase 40,000 of them to sell through my television program. Please rush me 40,000 albums. I will send you a check for them next week." I shouted all over that room.

Whatever You Have In Your Hand Is Enough To Start Your Next Miracle.

The profit enabled me to purchase a beautiful white Lincoln Town Car for cash! It launched an entire different season for my life and ministry. I was on air every time I drove up to a church for a crusade. Why? *I started with whatever was already in my hand.*

Last week, a lady wrote me a check for $5.00. She was embarrassed. She said, "I'm so ashamed to send you such a small check, but it's all that I have." I was reading her letter about 2:00 in the morning after coming in from a major meeting. My heart was so stirred. You see, what she was planting was *enough to impress God.*

He knows how much you have.

He knows how little you have.

Your obedience always secures His attention.

You don't have to write God a huge check for $100,000 to move His hand toward you. You simply have to obey the inner voice of the Holy Spirit with *whatever you presently possess.*

Remember the incredible scenario of the widow? "And Jesus sat over against the treasury, and beheld how the people cast money into the treasury: and many that were rich cast in much. And there came a certain poor widow, and she threw in two mites, which make a farthing. And he called unto him his disciples, and saith unto them, Verily I say unto you, That this poor widow hath cast more in, than all they which have cast into the treasury: For all they did cast in of their abundance; but she of her want did cast in all that she had, even all her living" (Mark 12:41-44).

She started her Harvest with what she had.

I have sowed jewelry, cars, clothes into other lives. I have planted hundreds of thousands of books and tapes as special Seeds. You see, *everything you have is a Seed.*

If you keep it today, that is your Harvest.

But if you release it, it becomes a Seed.

What you presently possess is only a Seed *if you sow it* into soil. When you keep it in your hand, it becomes the only Harvest you will ever have. Look around you. Is there a piece of furniture that a widow needs at her house? Could you volunteer two hours a week at your home church? That's a Seed.

Start with what you have.

Are you good at repairing automobiles? Discuss with your pastor your desire to repair the automobile of any widow in your congregation, as a Seed of Love.

You are a Walking Warehouse of Seeds. You have more inside you than you could ever imagine. But, you must take the time to inventory *everything* God has given you.

Do not permit pride to rob you of an opportunity to plant a Seed. When the offering plate is passed, even if you only possess $2.00 in your pocket — plant it.

Get your Harvest started.

As a parent, teach your child the importance of sowing something *consistently* in the work of God.

It may only be a dime or a quarter. But, they will create a flow and river of Harvest that will outlast every attack against their life.

Millions are waiting for more. They refuse to start their Harvest with a small Seed. It is one of the reasons they will never receive everything God wants to send to them. "Though thy beginning was small, yet thy latter end should greatly increase" (Job 8:7).

What you have will create anything else you want...if you *sow it.*

Let's pray:

"Father, show me the Seeds You have already given to me. I make a decision to sow any Seed You desire regardless of how small it now appears. You will multiply it back when I need it the most today. In Jesus' name. Amen."

❧ Mark 4:3-8 ❧

"Hearken; behold, there went out a sower to sow: And it came to pass, as he sowed, some fell by the way side, and the fowls of the air came and devoured it up. And some fell on stony ground where it had not much earth; and immediately it sprang up, because it had not depth of earth: But when the sun was up, it was scorched; and because it had no root, it withered away. Some fell among thorns, the thorns grew up and choked it, and it yielded not fruit. And other fell on good ground, and did yield fruit that sprang up and increased; and brought forth, some thirty, some sixty, and some an hundred."

≈ 23 ≈

SOME DO NOT KNOW THE DIFFERENCE BETWEEN GOOD SOIL AND BAD SOIL.

The Quality Of The Soil Affects The Seed.

That's why Jesus never invested time in debating with Pharisees. He was the Son of God. He knew it. It was *their* responsibility to discern it. He knew they were "fools and blind" (Matthew 23:17).

Yet, He took time to go home with the tax collector, Zacchaeus. You see, He discerned soil worthy of His attention and time.

Two thieves were crucified beside Christ. One received mercy. One did not. Why? The thief who believed in the Divinity of Jesus reached out. Jesus responded. *Both* thieves had needs. *Both* needed the miracle of salvation. But, Jesus took the time to respond to the one who reached out...*the good soil.*

Jesus taught the importance of observing the *quality of the soil.* "Hearken; behold, there went out a sower to sow: And it came to pass, as he sowed, some fell by the way side, and the fowls of the air came and devoured it up. And some fell on stony ground where it had not much earth; and immediately it sprung up, because it had no depth of earth: But when the sun was up, it was scorched; and because it had no root, it withered away. And some fell among thorns, and the thorns grew up, and choked it, and it yielded no fruit.

And others fell on good ground, and did yield fruit that sprang up and increased; and brought forth, some thirty, and some sixty, and some an hundred" (Mark 4:3-8).

Refuse to sow Seed into a non-giver. My treasured friend, Mack Timberlake, taught me this. Suppose you have a son-in-law that needs financial help. What do you do? Do you hand him money? Or, do you provide him *an opportunity* to earn it? There is a great difference. A lady approached me one night after a meeting and discussed her plight with me. Her son-in-law and daughter had been staying with her for several weeks.

"I feel so sorry for them. They are out of jobs. They need money. They are really going through a great financial trial at this time," she said tearfully.

"So, what does he do everyday at your home?"

"Well, they usually sleep in until 10:00 or so. Then, they watch television. They are waiting for doors to open," she explained.

"Does your daughter prepare your food while you are at work every day?" I asked.

"Oh no. She does not like to cook!"

"Does your son-in-law wash your dishes, clean your house, or has he waxed your car, mowed the grass while you are gone to work these days?"

"Well, he's kind of depressed right now. He really does not feel like working. And, I hate to ask him anyway," was her reply.

I showed her in the Scripture the

commandments that Paul wrote to the church at Thessalonica. "For even when we were with you, this we commanded you, that if any would not work, neither should he eat" (2 Thessalonians 3:10). He called those who did not work "disorderly" (2 Thessalonians 3:11).

The Apostle Paul instructed us to avoid having any fellowship with those who refuse to be productive. "And if any man obey not our word by this epistle, note that man, and have no company with him, that he may be ashamed" (2 Thessalonians 3:14).

Now, a lazy person is not necessarily your enemy. But, his unproductivity is to be noted, confronted, addressed and penalized (2 Thessalonians 3:15).

That's unproductive soil.

Refuse to sow Seed into a church that is against financial blessing. Why would I support any ministry that is in direct rebellion to the Laws of Provision according to Scripture?

Refuse to sow Seed into someone who refuses to work when doors open.

"Well, Mike, I am out of work."

Well, you might want to define that a little differently, since God has only promised to "bless all the work of thine hand" (Deuteronomy 28:12). You see, you can *find* work. *Anybody can find some kind of work.* It may not pay $40 an hour at first. It may not be the easiest thing you've ever done. But, work is everywhere you look in life.

Refuse to sow Seed in someone who is unteachable.

"I really need help. We cannot pay our bills.

Can you help us at this time?" one of my relatives asked me rather boldly one day.

"Let's sit down. I want to review your finances with you," I replied. "Give me a list of what you owe. Show me what you are doing to earn money. I'm going to give you some advice, and if you'll follow this advice, I will consider investing in you."

He did not have the time. Think about it! He did not have enough desire to prosper to even provide me a list of his bills and enter into a counseling session with me. He was unqualified to receive any Seed. *That's bad soil.* "Poverty and shame shall be to him that refuseth instruction: but he that regardeth reproof shall be honoured" (Proverbs 13:18).

Look for good soil continually. Now, there are many people near you that are good soil. Hundreds of ministries deserve your best Seed sowing. Look around you. Evaluate. Observe those who are productive around you. Boaz did this when he saw Ruth, he instructed servants to make it easier for her to secure a Harvest, "handfuls on purpose."

I love to sow Seed in young ministers. You see, they are emptying their lives into the gospel. Some have left good jobs and promise of fortune to help broken lives become healed. They do not have the rewards of momentum. Great reputations have not yet been established. I believe this produces great fruit.

I love to send money to ministers who are spreading this gospel of provision and prosperity. I know their warfare. They are despised by the world, misunderstood by the church, and fought by those who do not understand the message of prosperity.

So, I want to provide them Seed to keep this message of supernatural Harvest accessible to the hurting.

I love to sow Seed in proven ministries. They have fought a good fight. They have kept the faith. They have endured. *Endurance should be honored.*

"Mike, every time I plant a Seed in your ministry something happens in my ministry," a minister explained recently. Well, I really appreciated his statement, but I felt a little embarrassed. He continued. "Mike, there really is a difference when I sow Seed in *good soil.* It seems that my Harvest comes quickly, with great excellence, and I feel at peace about my Seed sowing."

Sow Seed into those *who have helped you.*

Sow Seed into those *who have given you wise counsel and correction.*

Sow Seed into the lives of those *who have stayed loyal and faithful.*

Sow Seed into those who are *willing to labor, toil and empty their life out for the cause of the gospel.* "And let us not be weary in well doing: for in due season we shall reap, if we faint not" (Galatians 6:9).

Many are not carefully choosing the soil where they sow their Seed. That's one of the reasons they will never reap the hundredfold return God would like for them to experience.

Let's pray:

"Father, where should I be sowing? Reveal the soil that will produce. Show me...I will not waste my Seed on unproductive soil. In Jesus' name. Amen."

⌇ Ecclesiastes 11:6 ⌇

"In the morning sow thy Seed, and in the evening withhold not thine hand: for thou knowest not whether shall prosper, either this or that, or whether they both shall be alike good."

❧ 24 ❧

SOME REFUSE TO SOW CONSISTENTLY.

When You Sow Continuously, Your Harvest Will *Become Continuous.*

When you sow inconsistently, your Harvest will become erratic. Many years ago I talked to a young couple after service. They were distraught. Discouraged. Blaming God for everything that happened in their life. When I approached the subject of tithing and sowing, they both jumped in with indignation.

"We have tried that already. It did not work for us."

It is a dangerous thing to call God a liar.

It shows a lack of the fear of God.

It reveals pride and arrogance. When you deliberately tell others that you have obeyed the Scriptures, and God's Word did not work for you, it is a dangerous and fearful thing.

"I would like to see your check stubs sometime," I countered. "I would like to see the *consistency* of your tithing. This is very important. If you have tithed and sowed Seed continuously for several months, through several seasons, this needs to be validated. Because the God I serve is not a liar. He said He would open the windows of heaven upon you. So, if you have missed any weeks of tithing, your

Harvest will become erratic and unpredictable."

They stuttered around. Then, they admitted that they had only "tried tithing" a few times. It was not the routine and pattern of their life. It was not their lifestyle.

Tithing is not an *experiment to be explored.*

Tithing is a *lifestyle of obedience.*

Observe the seasons. They are predictable. Winter, spring, summer, and fall create such regularity that we build our lives on the laws of this earth.

I sat in a remarkable seminar many years ago in Madrid, Spain. The scientist was explaining the distance and complications involved in landing a rocket on the moon. He stated that landing a rocket on the moon required such precision that it was the equivalent of a man *shooting a mosquito six miles away with a rifle.* Someone asked how would it be possible to do such a thing?

"Laws. This entire universe has specific laws that can be discovered when you cooperate with the Laws of the Universe. You can predict exactly where a rocket can be sent," he explained.

The ancient writer made it so clear, "To every thing there is a season, and a time to every purpose under the heaven: A time to be born, and a time to die; a time to plant, and a time to pluck up that which is planted... A time to get, and a time to lose; a time to keep, and a time to cast away...." (Read Ecclesiastes 3:1-8.)

You must learn the power of rhythm, routine and consistency. It is important to establish this in your sowing and reaping. Acknowledge that your life is an endless and continuous cycle of sowing and reaping, giving and receiving. Work with it. Don't work against it. Nature has a pattern. You can oppose it, hate it and despise it. But, the only way to reap the benefits and rewards is to observe and to cooperate with it.

Create a personal schedule for sowing Seeds into God's work. The Apostle Paul understood this principle. "Now concerning the collection for the saints, as I have given order to the churches of Galatia, even so do ye. *Upon the first day of the week* let every one of you lay by him in store, as God hath prospered him, that there be no gatherings when I come" (1 Corinthians 16:1, 2).

Reaping does not follow sowing. Waiting follows sowing.

You sow.

You wait.

You reap.

So, for you to experience a continuous incoming Harvest, there must be a *continuous sowing of Seed* to accommodate the seasons of waiting. As long as earth exists, seasons will exist. "While the earth remaineth, Seed time and Harvest, and cold and heat, and summer and winter, and day and night shall not cease" (Genesis 8:22).

Now, there are various reasons people refuse to sow consistently.

Their faith and confidence in God wavers. When they listen to a man of God with a specific anointing, they become responsive. As they sit under that anointing, faith comes alive within them. They get excited. Their faith is vibrant. Their confidence in God is renewed. Faith requires action. *It Is Almost Impossible To Sit Under A Man Of God Who Unlocks*

> **It Is Almost Impossible To Sit Under A Man Of God Who Unlocks The Flow Of Faith And Not Plant A Seed.**

The Flow Of Faith And Not Plant A Seed. In fact, it is a dangerous and tragic condition if you ever come to the place where you can sit under that kind of anointing and close your heart to it. So, it is only natural to become responsive to the *call of faith within you.* Some sneer at this. They have contempt and belittle this.

They call it "emotional giving."

I don't quite understand them. If God puts faith in your heart to plant a Seed, it is His nature rising up strong within you.

That desire to give *cannot be satanic.*

That desire to give *cannot be human.*

The desire to give is *the nature of God Himself.*

Some, a few days after they have been in the presence of God and His anointing, enter into conversion with those who lack faith. Critics. Scorners. The fearful.

"You were crazy to give an offering to that preacher. Don't you realize he will just buy a nice car and fancy clothes with your tithe and offering?" sneers the ungodly family of the faith-filled believer.

This kind of statement can poison your mind. Your heart becomes confused. Spiritual frustration sets in. You'll leave the Arena of Faith and enter into the *sewage of human debate.*

It is the quickest way to lose your Harvest. You see, your Harvest requires *faith,* not merely a Seed.

Your Seed is *what* you sow.

Your faith is *why* it multiplies.

God responds to your Seed *because it is wrapped*

with faith. He wants to be believed. He responds to faith *anywhere He finds it.* Even a sinner will get a miracle *when he believes.* This happened continuously in the Kathryn Kuhlman meetings. I have watched people get miracle after miracle. She would ask, "Are you a Christian?"

"No," came the hesitant replies.

Why would God heal a sinner? *Faith.* "Faith was reckoned to Abraham for righteousness." (Romans 4:9) "The word is nigh thee, even in thy mouth, and in thine heart: that is, the word of faith, which we preach;" (Romans 10:8).

So, don't expect an unsaved, rebellious and ungodly loved one to be excited when you plant a Seed into the work of God. They do not even appreciate Calvary yet. Jesus is unimportant to them. They sneer at the Scriptures. They are entangled in the tentacles of hell, like an octopus. They can purchase their liquor, cigarettes and gamble in the Casinos. But, when they find out their widowed mother gave money to a preacher, their fury will erupt like a volcano.

Refuse their intimidation and scorn.

The opinions of your friends will influence you. It matters. This is normal. However, do not expect someone unresponsive to the Holy Spirit and rebellious toward the principles of the Word of God to understand your sowing Seeds to spread the glorious gospel.

Doubt is not the only reason many refuse to sow with regularity. I have known of many people who get angry at a preacher and *hold their tithe back.*

"When my pastor does something to upset me, I simply stop paying my tithe," one lady said with fervor and anger. "God understands!"

You better know He understands. He understands your scorn, ingratitude and immaturity. You have not hurt your pastor when you withhold your tithe. You have not stopped the militant and victorious march of the church toward victory by withholding your tithe.

You have destroyed the supply line for your own family.

You have created *seasons of devastation* in your future. You have played the *part of a fool*. Satan fed you a lie. He baited the hook and like an ignorant fish, *you fell for it*.

Some stop sowing because they want to use the money for something special they want to purchase. They *intend* to pay it back. The car payment comes due. They see a refrigerator they want to buy. So, they talk themselves into *using the tithe* that week for personal use. *It's the quickest way to financial suicide.*

You cannot afford to *touch what belongs to God.*

You cannot afford to *keep what belongs to God.*

It is a lie from satan designed to maneuver you to a place of financial wipeout and devastation. Satan hates you. He despises you. He despises the flow of blessing in your life. That's why He was so angry about the blessings of Job.

Anything God *loves* is something satan *hates*.

Anything God *blesses* is something satan *curses*.

Others do not sow with regularity simply because they wait until they feel it. If I only gave when I felt it, I probably would not give very often. You see, my own needs often overwhelm me. When I look at a stack of television and radio bills, I can easily lose the "feeling" to go bless the work of God. In fact, I just saw an estimate to repair my roof this week. My house has been leaking for several weeks, and I've been too busy to get it repaired. (Or, maybe I just don't want to pay for it!) At any rate, as I look at the incredible cost of a new roof on my flat topped house, I lose every feeling and desire to write a check for the work of God!! It is the last thing I "feel like doing." You cannot afford to sow only as you are feeling it.

You must focus on *regularity.* "In the morning sow thy Seed, and in the evening withhold not thine hand: for thou knowest not whether shall prosper, either this or that, or whether they both shall be alike good" (Ecclesiastes 11:6). *Learn to sow into many ministries, not just one.* "Give *generously,* for your gifts will return to you later. Divide your gifts among many, for in the days ahead you yourself may need much help" (Ecclesiastes 11:1, 2 Living Bible).

I like the King James version of this, too. "Cast thy bread upon the waters: for thou shalt find it after many days. Give a portion to seven, and also to eight; for thou knowest not what evil shall be upon the earth" (Ecclesiastes 11:1, 2).

Some do not sow with regularity because they live in continuous crisis. When crisis comes, they quit giving. When blessing occurs, then they sow. If you sow according to your circumstances only, you will sow inconsistently. "He that observeth the wind shall not sow; and he that regardeth the clouds shall not reap" (Ecclesiastes 11:4).

Millions will stay in poverty because they refuse to enter the miracle of *consistent* sowing.

≈ Deuternonomy 28:47,48 ≈

"Because thou servedst not the Lord thy
God with joyfulness, and with gladness of
heart, for the abundance of all things,
therefore shalt thou serve thine enemies
which the Lord shall send against thee, in
hunger, and in thirst, and in nakedness,
and in want of all things: and he shall put a
yoke of iron upon thy neck, until he have
destroyed thee."

≈ 25 ≈

MILLIONS ARE UNTHANKFUL AND DO NOT APPRECIATE WHAT GOD HAS ALREADY GIVEN TO THEM.

Thankfulness Is A Force.

It is more than an attitude. It is a lifestyle, a way of life. It is a way of looking at things. *It is impossible to be too thankful throughout life.*

Thankfulness is a learned attitude. It is not necessarily something born inside you. I have watched unthankful people make turnarounds *after a crisis.* Suddenly, their words of appreciation are effusive and many because they have memories of lack, pain and losses. He who God has forgiven much is thankful for much, was the implication of Jesus regarding Mary Magdalene. (See Luke 7:36-50.)

Thankfulness is magnetic. When you work around someone who is thankful, they are happy.

Thankful people are always joyous people. It doesn't mean that their life is free from stress, heartache, or difficulties. But rather they have chosen to focus on the wonder and the miracle of blessing.

Thankfulness is created by focus (Deuteronomy 8:10-14).

Thankfulness is required for entering the presence of God. "Enter into His gates with thanksgiving, and into His courts with praise: be thankful unto Him, and bless His name" (Psalm 100:4).

Thankfulness should occur because of the goodness of God, not because perfect circumstances. "Be thankful unto Him, and bless His name. For the Lord is good; His mercy is everlasting; and His truth endureth to all generations" (Psalm 100:4, 5).

You are commanded to be thankful. "In everything give thanks: for this is the will of God in Christ Jesus concerning you" (1 Thessalonians 5:18).

Thankfulness occurs when you begin to remember good things God has done for you. "We give thanks to God always for you all...remembering without ceasing your work of faith, and labor of love, and patience and hope in our Lord Jesus Christ..." (1 Thessalonians 1:2, 3).

You must replay the memories of God's blessings in your life. He is a good God. He is a powerful God. He is a loving God.

He has brought you through *the fire.*

He has brought you through *the flood.*

He has preserved you through *false accusations.*

He has walked in *when others walked out.*

You are serving a miracle, loving and powerful God. If nothing else good ever occurred in your life, His presence is enough to inspire gratitude, appreciation, and thankfulness.

Sing your gratitude and thankfulness to God. Compose songs. They do not have to be fancy, articulate and profound words. He just wants to hear you sing praise and worship to Him.

Write notes of thankfulness and gratitude to God and those you love. Five minutes with a handwritten note will unlock a river within you. Suddenly, you will remember all the wonderful things God has done for you.

Unthankful people are not replaying the right memories. "Remember ye not the former things, neither consider the things of old. Behold, I will do a new thing; now it shall spring forth; shall ye not know it? I will even make a way in the wilderness, and rivers in the desert" (Isaiah 43:18, 19).

Gratitude is a gift to those you love. "Withhold not good from them to whom it is due, when it is in the power of thine hand to do it" (Proverbs 3:27).

What you are most thankful about will begin to multiply in your life. When you are thankful for friends, you will multiply your friendships. When you are thankful for the opportunity your boss gives you, money will begin to increase in your life.

The proof of thankfulness is joy and the willingness to protect. You will protect and fight for the things for which you are most thankful. Have you ever seen a mother race across the yard when a dog approached her child? That protectiveness came because of her thankfulness and appreciation for her child. Her baby is her life. *You will always fight to keep what you truly love.* When an employee is thankful, they'll fight to keep their job. You won't find them coming late to work, taking extra time away during the lunch hour. Why? They're grateful. Thankful.

Unthankfulness is a dangerous cancer that can

enter so quickly. It comes when a contentious loved one and friend fuels a misunderstanding. They feed your anger. Something upsets you. Your focus is broken. Husbands and wives can feed each other's agitation. The wife is angry because the boss requested overtime. The husband ponders and meditates and receives the offense as well. Within weeks, they cannot look the boss in the eye. When a fellow employee shares their complaint, they add theirs with it.

Unthankfulness is contagious. I walked off the plane recently with great joy. My life was going wonderful. The ministry was touched by God. The finances were up. I simply felt good. Two minister friends of mine were waiting. They suggested a meal, and I agreed. Within moments, they began to share some of the trials they were going through. My heart filled with compassion. I listened. They continued and suddenly almost without warning, I was in a completely different arena. I heard myself discussing things I should never have discussed. I shared my trials, my complaints, and those who had failed me. Within two hours from my arrival, my heart was in such turmoil and frustration I could not explain it.

What had happened? I had permitted my focus to be broken. Unthankful people had entered my presence. I permitted it, allowed it, and even fed it. My joy left. My enthusiasm waned.

Yet nothing had really changed in my entire life except my attitude.

You see, somebody is speaking into your life continuously. *An unthankful person can wreck the flow of miracles into your life incredibly.*

Here are a few helpful keys in staying thankful

and teachable during seasons of financial crisis:

1. *Recognize unthankfulness as a sin and grievous to the Holy Spirit.* "And grieve not the Holy Spirit of God, whereby ye are sealed until the day of redemption" (Ephesians 4:30).

2. *Stop discussing anything that does not build up another.* "Let no corrupt communication proceed out of your mouth, but that which is good to the use of edifying, that it may minister grace unto the hearers" (Ephesians 4:29).

3. *Focus on the wonderful blessings so evident and obvious in your life.* "Blessed be the Lord, who daily loadeth us with benefits, even the God of our salvation" (Psalm 68:19).

4. *Cry out to God when you sense an unthankful spirit growing.* "The righteous cry, and the Lord heareth, and delivereth them out of all their troubles" (Psalm 34:17).

5. *Confess your sin of ingratitude with a broken and contrite heart.* "The Lord is nigh unto them that are of a broken heart; and saveth such as be of a contrite spirit" (Psalm 34:18).

6. *Believe your trial will cease and God will give you full deliverance.* "Many are the afflictions of the righteous: but the Lord delivereth him out of them all. He keepeth all his bones: not one of them is broken" (Psalm 34:19, 20).

7. *Keep a picture of the miracle you are pursuing in front of you at all times.* "Forgetting those things which are behind, and reaching forth unto those things which are before, I press toward the mark for the prize of the high calling of God in Christ Jesus" (Philippians 3:13, 14).

8. *Withdraw from unthankful and contentious*

people. "Evil communications corrupt good manners" (1 Corinthians 15:33). "As coals are to burning coals, and wood to fire; so is a contentious man to kindle strife" (Proverbs 26:21).

Unthankfulness blinds you to every gift of God. You become critical, cynical and fault finding. You refuse to be thankful for your car because you see your neighbor drive up in a new one.

Ingratitude can be cured. I have found two major methods God deals with unthankfulness.

His first choice is for you to *enter the Secret Place,* beholding His goodness and becoming thankful in His presence. It is impossible to habitually enter your private place of prayer, praising and worshipping Him, and remain unthankful when you leave.

The second method for dealing with unthankfulness is devastating. *Loss Is The Best Cure For Unthankfulness.* God simply takes away something you are not thankful for. "Because thou servest not the Lord thy God with joyfulness, and with gladness of heart, for the abundance of all things; Therefore shalt thou serve thine enemies which the Lord shall send against thee, in hunger, and in thirst, and in nakedness, and in want of all things: and he shall put a yoke of iron upon thy neck, until he have destroyed thee" (Deuteronomy 28:47, 48).

> *Loss Is The Best Cure For Unthank-fulness.*

Unthankful people are often militant influencing others with their ingratitude. They're not satisfied to sit at home alone. They do not want to eat alone in restaurants. They cannot thrive alone. *Their unthankfulness requires fuel.* They pursue others to sow their Seeds of contention, discord and strife. If you do not remove them from your life, you will enter into a covenant with them, thus *destroying every blessing God is trying to place near you.*

Unthankful people create an atmosphere of discouragement. Motivation is drained in their presence. You lose energy. The projects that excited you suddenly look too impossible to achieve. You start looking at hurdles instead of potential blessings. They are burdens not burden-bearers.

Unthankful people demotivate you. They demoralize you and destroy every dream of God within you.

You cannot afford the tragedy of an unthankful person in your life.

Ingratitude and lack of appreciation for what God has already done is one of the most important reasons people will never taste the one hundredfold return.

Please pray with me:

"Jesus, forgive my unthankfulness. I see how deadly ingratitude can be. I purpose to remember Your goodness, Your grace and Your miracles. Cleanse me. I will sing a new song of thankfulness and those who come close to me will hear about Your greatness and Your goodness. I shall prosper and experience Your Harvest. In Jesus' name. Amen."

≈ Proverbs 22:24,25 ≈

"Make no friendship with an angry man;
and with a furious man thou shalt not go:
Lest thou learn his ways, and get a snare to
thy soul."

⁓ 26 ⁓

Most People Fail To Recognize The Enemies Of Their Harvest And Prosperity.

Everything Good Has An Enemy.

Jesus had an enemy. So, you will have an enemy throughout your entire lifetime. "The disciple is not above his master, nor the servant above his Lord" (Matthew 10:24).

> **Everything Good Has An Enemy.**

Your enemy is any person or influence that endeavors to stop you from achieving a worthy dream or goal assigned by God. Your enemy will use words, delays and attacks to drain your energy and change your focus. Now, satan is your true enemy. He uses people as *Instruments of Distraction.* His goal does not end with your devastation.

His goal is to rob God of the pleasure you generate. The eyes of the Lord are always upon you. He delights in your progress, peace and fellowship. What was the goal of satan in the Garden of Eden? To stop the pleasure God experienced in fellowshipping with Adam and Eve.

Your enemy fears you. Satan is so aware of the

plans of God. He fully recognizes your potential and what God is planning for your life. He attacks out of fear of your success. You have the relationship he formerly enjoyed with God. David saw this happen in his own life. "And Saul was afraid of David, because the Lord was with him, and was departed from Saul" (1 Samuel 18:12).

Your Enemy Is To Be Destroyed, Not Understood. God has numbered satan's days. Even David departed when he saw the envy and jealousy of Saul's attacks. (1 Samuel 18:12).

Never negotiate with an enemy. "Make no friendship with an angry man; and with a furious man thou shalt not go: Lest thou learn his ways, and get a snare to thy soul" (Proverbs 22:24, 25).

Move away from a climate of conflict whenever possible. This was one of the Master Leadership Secrets of David. He understood the importance of protecting his own focus in his dealings with King Saul. "And David avoided out of his presence twice" (1 Samuel 18:11).

Do not fuel and energize your enemy. Your very presence and words often breathe energy and strength into your enemy unless they are the right words. "A soft answer turneth away wrath: but grievous words stir up anger" (Proverbs 15:1).

You cannot solve a problem for your enemy. His goal is to destroy you. You are the object of his attention.

Your dream is your goal.

Your destruction is his goal.

Achieving your Assignment and completing

instructions from God is your goal. Destroying you is his focus. "Wrath is cruel, and anger is outrageous; but who is able to stand before envy?" (Proverbs 27:4).

Your enemy will not invest any time, money or effort to understand and embrace your Assignment on earth. The Pharisees attempted to use the very explanations of Jesus to entrap him. Jesus knew this. Their questions were "hooks" to side track Him and break His focus. That's why He answered their questions with another question.

The motives of others should help you to give the kinds of answers you give them.

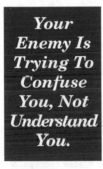

Your Enemy Is Trying To Confuse You, Not Understand You.

Your enemy must be discerned early. "Neither give place to the devil" (Ephesians 4:27).

Continuous conflict reveals the presence of an enemy you are permitting. "For where envying and strife is, there is confusion and every evil work" (James 3:16).

Your enemy seeks dialogue, exchange and communication instead of a solution. "Ever learning, and never able to come to the knowledge of the truth" (2 Timothy 3:7).

Your enemy will not show mercy. This is the proof that Wisdom is not present. "But the Wisdom that is from above is...peaceable...easy to be entreated, full of mercy" (James 3:17).

Your financial Harvest has an enemy. "The thief cometh not, but for to steal, and to kill, and to destroy" (John 10:10). Job experienced this when satan appeared in the presence of God and desired to destroy his life.

Face your enemy immediately. Name things for what they really are. What you are unwilling to confront, you become unqualified to conquer. Champions fight back. Become serious about winning against poverty and lack. I have said it many times: financial Harvest is not a frivolous thing of trivia. It is hell's biggest fear of the church in this generation.

Let's look at three enemies that destroy your financial Harvest.

1. *Wrong Relationships.*

Your friends are fueling your dream or your doubts.

Your friends are either energizing you or attacking you. You must decide and *discern* those satan is using to destroy your financial Harvest. "He that walketh with wise men shall be wise: but a companion of fools shall be destroyed" (Proverbs 13:20).

> **Someone You Love Is Often Listening To Someone Else.**

Some friends are *parasites*, draining you in every conceivable way.

Some friends are *encouragers*, imparting to you remarkable energy and enthusiasm for the Harvest ahead.

Some *envy* you and will criticize you as materialistic and a lover of money.

Some will *compete with you.* They will be miserable and upset when your creativity explodes.

Some friends will *doubt you.* They will point out every reason you can expect failure.

The Apostle Paul warned. "And have no fellowship with the unfruitful works of darkness, but rather reprove them" (Ephesians 5:11).

But if you fail, you will fail because you permitted the wrong people to come too close. Read the biography of great men who experienced terrible failures.

They trusted the wrong people.

2. *Wrong Teaching.*

Somebody is always imparting wrong information. It will affect you and influence you more than you realize. The Apostle Paul recognized that those he loved were listening to *someone else.* "Oh foolish Galatians, who hath bewitched you, that ye should not obey the truth?" (Galatians 3:1).

Error is *deadly.* It's poisonous. It is always mixed with the threads of half-truth. This keeps it deceitful.

One of the greatest errors being taught today is regarding the *Sovereignty of God.* It is so misunderstood. Let me explain.

"Don't you feel that satan gives you a lot of money so you will backslide and get away from God?" asked a serious young businessman one night after a lecture.

"Let me ask you a question," I replied. "If financial wealth could break your relationship with God, don't you feel that satan would overdose you every day of your life?" He saw the point.

I continued, "When satan wanted to destroy Job, he didn't increase his income. He stopped the money flow into his life."

Another lady spoke up one day, "If God wanted us to have money, He would give it to us."

I answered, "Does that mean if God wanted you to comb your hair, He would have combed it for you this morning? If God wanted you to wear clothes, you would not have been born naked?"

Another sharp and articulate businessman spoke up at a conference. "Well, I believe that God will give you money if He can trust you with it."

"Then explain to me why many ungodly, atheistic men have millions, and missionaries cannot even buy vehicles for their ministry if this is a trust factor with God?" I answered.

Oh, it is so tragic! When I hear the responses of people regarding financial blessing and wealth, millions make no effort at all to learn and apply themselves to the Principle of Increase. Then, they are puzzled when their money never grows and they stay in abject poverty.

3. *Wrong Words.*

Your words are creative. They are powerful. They are currents that are rushing you toward your dream or away from your dream. "Death and life are in the power of the tongue: and they that love it shall eat the fruit thereof" (Proverbs 18:21).

Your words can sabotage productive and rewarding friendships. "Whoso keepeth his mouth and his tongue keepeth his soul from troubles" (Proverbs 21:23).

Your words decide what grows within you. "The mouth of a righteous man is a well of life" (Proverbs 10:11).

Your words can create unnecessary and destructive anger in others. "A soft answer turneth away wrath: but grievous words stir up anger" (Proverbs 15:1).

Your words can set traps that destroy you. "A fool's mouth is his destruction, and his lips are the snare of his soul" (Proverbs 18:7).

Your words should be spoken at the appropriate time and place. "A fool uttereth all his mind: but a wise man keepeth it in till afterwards" (Proverbs 29:11).

Your words can be the vehicle to your own deliverance from a dilemma. "The mouth of the upright shall deliver them" (Proverbs 12:6).

Your words deserve much forethought before releasing them. "The heart of the righteous studieth to answer" (Proverbs 15:28).

You must be careful who qualifies to receive your spoken opinion and advice. "Speak not in the ears of a fool: for he will despise the Wisdom of thy words" (Proverbs 23:9).

Your words are deciding your seasons. Your words are deciding your energy and enthusiasm. Your words that come out of your own mouth are creating a path to your future or a current to your past.

Stop discussing your flaws with everyone. Stop advertising the mistakes you have made. Stop discussing your doubts and advertising your fears.

You are a giant killer, a champion, a repairer and a restorer of dreams. Talk like it. Act like it.

Thousands continuously poison their own environment with negative, doubting and fearful words. It's one of the reasons they will never taste their financial Harvest.

Nobody wants to invest in someone planning on losing. Your mouth is:

▶ Your Deliverer.

▶ Your Weapon.

▶ Your Motivator.

Use it wisely.

204 ■ *MIKE MURDOCK*

Millions refuse to acknowledge their enemies of prosperity. They will never taste the sweetness of financial provision.

Let's pray:

"Father, take unproductive, unholy and unthankful people out of my life. Uproot any error I have embraced ignorantly. Pour Your Words of faith and victory through me. In Jesus' name. Amen."

❧ 27 ❧

MILLIONS ARE NOT EXPERIENCING INCREASE BECAUSE NOBODY HAS YET TOLD THEM ABOUT THE PRINCIPLE OF SEED-FAITH.

The Unlearned Are Simply Untaught.

Teachers are necessary. You would not have the ability to even read this book, but a teacher entered your life. You sat at their feet. You learned the alphabet. Hour after hour you sat through boring, agitating and often frustrating moments. But, it opened the Golden Door to Life.

You can only know something you have heard. Something you have been taught. That is why God gives mentors, ministers of the gospel, and parents to impart knowledge. "And He gave some, apostles; and some, prophets; and some, evangelists; and some, pastors and teachers; For the perfecting of the saints, for the work of the ministry, for the edifying of the body of Christ...That we henceforth be no more children, tossed to and fro, and carried about with every wind of doctrine" (Ephesians 4:11,12,14).

Everyone understands sowing. Sowing is planting a Seed in soil for a desired Harvest and return.

Seed-Faith is sowing a specific Seed in faith that it will grow a Harvest throughout your life. It is deciding what kind of Harvest you want to grow and sowing a Seed to *make it happen.*

Seed-Faith is letting go of something you have been given to create something else you have been promised.

Seed-Faith is using something you have to create something else you want. When you let go of what is in your hand, God will let go of what is in His hand.

Your Seed is what blesses somebody else.

Your Harvest is anything that blesses you.

So, *Seed-Faith is sowing something you possess in faith that God will honor it by bringing a Harvest where you need it most.*

Now, most people have never understood the wonderful, glorious part of this principle of sowing and reaping. In fact, it is usually a threat. You will hear a parent tell a rebellious teenager, "Some day, you're going to reap what you sow!" Now, they rarely say that to the teenager when he is obedient and doing something wonderful! They only emphasize that when they are focusing on something *wrong* that their child did.

Every minister has used Galatians 6:7 to motivate their congregation to have a healthy fear of God. "Be not deceived; God is not mocked: for whatsoever a man soweth, that shall he also reap." But, if you keep reading after that verse, it is a wonderful and powerful promise that concludes, "...but he that soweth to the Spirit shall of the Spirit reap life everlasting. And let us not be weary in well doing: for in due season we shall reap, if we faint not" (Galatians 6:7-9).

The Apostle Paul continues emphasizing this incredible and miraculous principle of Seed-Faith. It is his personal encouragement in using this principle to help people *do something wonderful for others!* "As we have therefore opportunity, let us do good unto all men, especially unto them who are of the household of faith" (Galatians 6:10).

The principle of sowing and reaping in Scripture is a threat. It is also a wonderful and glorious *promise* to believers that *patience in sowing Seed will produce a Harvest worthy of pursuit.*

The principle: You can decide any Harvest you would like to reap and sow a special Seed, wrapped with your faith, for a desired result.

This is Seed-Faith.

God works this principle *continually.* Here's an example: He had a Son, Jesus. But, He wanted a family. So, He planted His best Seed on a place called Calvary to produce a glorious family, the body of Christ. Here we are!

Elijah, the remarkable prophet, understood this principle as much as any other person in Scripture. He looks in the face of an impoverished peasant woman about to eat her last meal. Her son is shriveled and withered, emaciated, laying in the bed. She is destitute. This is not simply a widow needing more money to make a car note, or pay for her house. Her last piece of bread is the only thing between her and starvation.

But, God has smiled on her. Oh, He did not send her a bag of groceries! (You see, even a bag of groceries would have an end to it.) Elijah did not hand her a $20 bill. That would merely delay starvation a few more hours.

Something In Your Hand Is Your Bridge Out Of Trouble.

God sent her a man who understood *how to keep creating Harvest after Harvest with a simple Seed.* Oh, it is a marvelous day in your life when God sends someone who can see the future of your Seed! You have found favor with angels! You have found favor that will outlast your present trial! You may be staring at your "present" with total discouragement, but that man of God has a *picture of your future.*

Elijah did not say, "I will tell the church about your problem and see if anyone can help you." He did not criticize her. He did not ask her if she had been tithing. He pointed to something *she already had* and told her how to use it as *a bridge out of trouble.*

You see, your Seed is the *only exit* from your present. Your Seed is the *only door* into your future.

Your Seed is the *bridge of blessing* into the world you have dreamed about your entire life.

Elijah did something glorious and wonderful. Something I wish every man of God would do when he stands behind his pulpit and talks to people about an offering for the work of God. He explained that what she already had in her hand *contained the solution to her life.*

Seed-Faith is bringing people beyond the porch of their problem and bringing them into the House of Wisdom, and showing them that every solution to their life is right there in their own hand!

The unconverted can feel empty and hopeless. But, God teaches that the Seed for their salvation is already in their mouth. "The word is nigh thee, even in thy mouth, and in thy heart: that is, the word of faith, which we preach; That if thou shalt confess with thy mouth the Lord Jesus, and shalt believe in thine heart that God hath raised Him from the dead, thou shalt be saved. For with the heart man believeth unto righteousness; and with the mouth confession is made unto salvation" (Romans 10:8-10).

Think about it! You may be backslidden, broken, tormented and burdened down. Your sins number into the hundreds. Yet, right where you sit this very moment *you can plant a Seed*. What is the Seed? *Your confession of Christ*. In a single second, millions have moved from a life of emptiness and hopelessness into light and joy. *A single Seed of confession can bring a man out of trouble for the rest of his life*.

That is Seed-Faith. The glorious principle of Seed-Faith. Everybody believes in sowing. *Few* have embraced the promise of the Harvest!

Some have not taught it because they fear criticism. You see, when you begin to talk about money, you are focusing on the core of people's lives. Money is the god of this world. *Everything* revolves around it. Powerful ministries avoid this topic like the plague. Yet, in the privacy of their leadership sessions, they weep and intercede for God to provide more finances so they can reach this generation.

Some, refusing to discuss the principle of sowing and reaping often approach the wealthy in the privacy of their homes. There, they request and ask for large donations for their ministry. Through this means, they deflect any criticism that could come from public emphasis.

Some feel that it is unbalanced to talk about money in a church service. Yet, nobody considers a dentist unbalanced because he works only on teeth. Nobody considers a lawyer unbalanced because he only discusses legal matters.

Nobody becomes angry at an evangelist for preaching salvation. Few become furious with a pastor teaching on the principles of loving relationships. Everyone gets excited when thousands receive their healing in a miracle service.

But, the moment money is discussed, *another spirit enters the arena.* The atmosphere *changes.* The climate is *different.*

Some do not teach on the principles of prosperity because their own supply is sufficient. Recently, I walked into a million dollar home. It was the residence of a minister friend. He never preaches on financial prosperity. Souls are his focus. He is brilliant at building homes for a profit. He has friends who build a home. He moves in. Later, when he sells it, he makes a generous profit. Over the years, he has made a tremendous amount of money. He has no financial problems whatsoever because of his gift of building. He understands contracting, and everything that goes along with it.

Many do not have this knowledge and background. So, while he enjoys the beautiful luxury of his million dollar home, thousands sit under his ministry who can hardly make their car payment. Their homes are tiny, cramped, and uncomfortable. You see, *supply is not his focus any more.* So, it has never dawned on him that others have a problem he does not have.

Some do not teach about sowing for a Harvest because of the anger, retaliation and fierce attack that it attracts to their ministry. Nobody who wants to be productive has time for battle. Several years ago a powerful minister ministered to millions on television. When the media began to set a trap and strategy to destroy him, it cost him millions in lawyer fees. His staff became so fragmented. Their focus was broken. Instead of writing books that helped people, he had to meet with lawyers for hundreds of hours. His tax records were analyzed. Investigators searched through garbage containers to find financial documents and letters from partners.

The ungodly will invest millions to shut the mouth of one man of God. So, many men of God will avoid this teaching *so they can retain their focus* on people instead of defending their ministry. It's costly. It's devastating, physically and spiritually.

Consequently, their people plunge into poverty and loss because *they remain untaught.*

Something intrigues me. When the discussion of money and giving to the work of God emerges, *the ungodly find a common ground with many religious leaders.* They join together — like Pontius Pilate did with the Pharisees of his day for the common goal of crucifying Jesus of Nazareth.

Why is there anger over the message of sowing Seed to create a financial Harvest in your personal life?

Do these people despise giving? I don't think so. You see, our entire earth is a giving earth. Thousands give to the March of Dimes, Muscular Dystrophy telethons, the Red Cross, and the

Salvation Army. Nobody is angry about your giving...*to other people.* Their anger involves giving *to the work of God.*

Are they angry because teaching on prosperity is unnecessary and wasted time? Of course not. Most people do not have enough money to pay their present bills. Most do not even have a car that is paid for. Someone has said 60 percent of Americans would be bankrupt within 90 days if their job were stopped or terminated. No, the anger is not because everyone has too much money. Everyone is needy.

Is the anger directed toward all the ministers of the gospel for receiving offerings? I don't believe so. I see many ministers on television who are not criticized when they simply announce that there is a need for an offering so they can build a cathedral. The greatest evangelist of our generation receives offerings in every crusade. He has never been criticized, because his offerings are very low key.

No, the anger is not over receiving offerings. That has gone on for hundreds of years. The anger is not over a church that needs help or widows who need assistance.

Do those who fight the Seed-Faith message of prosperity despise money and hate the subject of money? Not at all. I watched a talk show host recently blast his anger fiercely at others who talked about sowing to get prosperity. Yet he offered his own video at the end of his program for $40. So, he does not hate money. He wants more of it for himself. He is not anti-money. He certainly is not against making a profit.

Those who become infuriated over sowing toward prosperity are angry that a minister promises a *hundredfold return from God for their Seed*. They hate the teaching that you can "give something you have and get something back in return from God."

The battle is over Expectation of a Harvest.

Let's analyze this. Are they angry because they believe God *can not* give a Harvest? Most people believe God can do anything.

The Anti-Prosperity Cult Despises The Teaching On Faith And Expectation Of A Harvest— The Only Pleasure God Receives From Man.

Do these believe that God *should not* produce a Harvest from our Seed? I don't think so. Every television reporter searches for impoverished ghetto areas to stir up the consciousness of America toward the poor. Thousands even get angry at God for not doing something for them. Most every human believes God should prosper him.

Do they believe that God *will not* really prosper people who sow into His work?

Now, there is a lot of controversy over this.

Here is one of the greatest discoveries of my life. The anger over sowing Seed into the work of God to get a Harvest arises because many believe it is wrong to expect something back from God.

The hated word is *expectation*.

"When I give to God, I expect nothing in return!" bragged one religious leader recently. "I give because I love Him. I give because of obedience. It is greedy to expect something back in return." Yet, this same religious leader expects a paycheck every single week of his life — in return for his spiritual leadership.

It is only expecting *money* back from God that produces the point of contention.

Is it wrong to give your heart to God and expect forgiveness, mercy, and a home in heaven? Oh, no! That's all right to expect an eternal home in return. Is it wrong to bring your sick body to God and expect Divine healing in return? Few disagree with that.

It is only money that bothers them. Money given to God and His work.

Why is it wrong to expect God to give a hundredfold return? This is not even logical. Think of the hundreds of doctrines taught in the Scriptures. The doctrine of the blood, the Holy Spirit, angels and demons. Think of the horrifying consequences of sin, rebellion, and witchcraft. If there should be rebellion to something taught in Scripture, why have we chosen to hate the Principle of Prosperity? It is against every part of our logic to hate something that brings blessing, provision, and ability to bless others.

This is a satanic thing. Oh, my friend, if you could see satan for what he really is, you would despise him with every ounce of your being. He is slimy, slick, and deceptive. He truly is a serpent.

Why isn't there great anger and hatred over the preaching on hell? If I were going to refuse truth, it would be the belief in a hell. You see, it is not even natural to be anti-money.

Suppose you and I were shopping. As we walked through the mall, I saw a man huddled in the corner.

"Oh, there's a man who needs help. He looks hungry. His clothes look tattered. Let's do something good for him." You and I walk over to him.

"Sir, are you all right?"

"No," he mutters. "I have not eaten in four days. I am out of work, and unemployed. I am homeless. Can you help me in any way?"

You and I rejoice. Here is our chance to bless this man. "Here, sir. Here is $20. Please buy yourself a good meal at the cafeteria."

Now suppose this happened. He takes the $20 bill. He tears it in pieces. He looks up at us angrily, "Why are you trying to give me a $20 bill?"

You would call this insanity. I would agree. I would say, "Here's a very sick man. He threw away something that could change his pain into pleasure. I handed him an answer, a solution, some money. He acts like it is a trap, a trick, poison."

Yet, the great Provider of this universe hands us the Principle of Prosperity that will rewrite our financial future, and we erupt with anger at the thought that we could sow a Seed and reap a Harvest!

This is insanity!

It is not insanity of the mind, it is insanity of the will, the *chosen* path of rebellion.

Are we against money? Of course not. When we find a quarter on the pavement, we tell every friend on the telephone that day. When we discover a $20 bill forgotten in the pocket of our old clothes in the corner of our closet, we shout! It brings fresh motivation into us. Maybe it doesn't take a lot to excite us these days — just the unexpected.

The entire warfare over the Seed-Faith message and the principles of prosperity is over this — *Expectation of a Financial Harvest back from God.*

Now, here is the most incredible truth: Expectation is the only pleasure man can generate in the *heart of God.*

You see, faith is confidence in God.

Expectation is the evidence of your faith.

God said that it is impossible to pleasure Him *unless you expect something from Him.* "But without faith it is impossible to please Him: for He that cometh to God must believe that He is, and that He is a rewarder of them that diligently seek Him" (Hebrews 11:6).

You cannot even be saved *unless you expect Him* to receive you.

You cannot be healed unless you *expect Him* to heal you.

You cannot be changed unless you *expect Him* to change you.

His only *pleasure* is to be *believed.*

His only *pain* is to be *doubted.*

I'll say it again, the essence of the entire Bible is Numbers 23:19: "God is not a man, that He should lie; neither the son of man, that He should repent: hath He said, and shall He not do it? or hath He spoken, and shall He not make it good?"

God is not a man.

Man lies. *God doesn't.*

Think about this! God is not pleasured by streets of gold, clouds of angels. He is only happy when somebody is *expecting Him to do what He said.*

What is believing? *Expecting God to do something He promised.*

This huge controversy is not even about you or your home. Your poverty is not the goal of satan. You are not the real enemy to him.

God is the enemy of satan.

Satan knows what pleasures God — for a human to trust Him, believe Him, depend on Him.

Satan remembers the presence of God. He is a former employee.

He is an angel who refused to believe God and is tasting the eternal consequences.

The goal of satan is to rob God of every moment of pleasure received from humans.

How can he rob God? *When he stops your expectation of a miracle, he has paralyzed and stopped the only pleasure God experiences.* Every time you expect a miracle, you create a river of pleasure through the heart of God. Every time you doubt, you create waves of pain. God has feelings too.

That is what is behind the *anti-prosperity cult* on earth.

They are not anti-money.

They are not against your having money.

They are against you expecting any money from God.

Oh, my precious friend, listen to my heart today. Why would men waste time, precious expensive television time, smearing, sneering and destroying other men of God who are praying for people to get out of poverty? This world is impoverished. Somebody said that forty percent of bankruptcies involve born-again Christians. This world is experiencing a financial crush every day. You would think that everyone would praise, admire and encourage any man of God who wanted to see them blessed, pay their bills, and send their children through college. Why aren't we thanking God aloud and often for the wonderful teaching that our Jehovah is a miracle God of provision?

It is not the teaching that you can have money that is bothering them.

It is the teaching that *God will supply you a Harvest when you release your Seed to Him.*

When you involve "the expectation of a return" with an offering, you arouse every devil in hell who despises their former boss who is pleasured by your expectation.

They hate the God you love.

They are obsessed with *depriving Him of every possible moment of pleasure* you are creating in the heart of God.

Your Father simply wants to *be believed.* That's all. He just wants to be believed. In fact, He promised that if you would just put Him above everything else in your life, He would keep providing anything you needed *for the rest of your life* (Matthew 6:33). *He wants to be believed.* He invited you to prove His Word to you (Malachi 3:9-11).

Here is the argument of the anti-prosperity cult. "What about greed? That is materialism. When you offer some money back for giving to God, that is satanic. That is ungodly! That is poisonous and deceptive to offer something back when you give to God."

Then, *why did God offer us something back in return for Seed, if that is greed?* Do you feel that it is greedy to work for a salary? You are getting something in return!

God anticipated greed. He knew our need and desire for increase could be deceptive, distorted, and easily used by satan to manipulate us. So, He built in a "corrective."

He put something in the system of increase that would completely remedy and cure any problem with greed — GIVING.

It is impossible for you to give to God and *stay* greedy.

That's why He established the tithing system of returning ten percent back to Him.

That's why He promised Peter a hundredfold return for giving up everything to follow Christ (Mark 10:28-30).

Every person who sows their Seed has just conquered greed.

Greed hoards.

God gives.

It is impossible to give your way to greed.

Now, inside of each of us is an invisible command to become more, to multiply and *increase.* The *first commandment* ever given by God in the Book of Genesis was to multiply and replenish and *become more.*

God is a God of Increase. It is normal to become more, *desire* more and *produce* more. Remember the story regarding the man with one talent? He was punished eternally. Why? He did not do anything with his gifts and skills to increase his life. In fact, what he had was given to another person who had multiplied, used his gifts, and become productive.

God is not cruel. He is not a liar and deceptive. If He gives you a desire for increase and prosperity, *He will place something inside you that can correct the problem it produces.* Giving.

All the preaching against greed and materialism *is only necessary for non-tithers and non-givers.*

Any discussion with the giver becoming greedy is totally unnecessary. His Seed is proof he has conquered it. His Seed is the corrective to potential greed.

What you can walk away from is something you have mastered. What you cannot walk away from is something that has mastered *you.*

Weeping will not correct greed.

Screaming will not correct it.

Confession will not stop greed.

Sowing Is The Only Known Cure For Greed.

> **Sowing Is The Only Known Cure For Greed.**

Obedience. Just returning the tithe. Just replanting the Seed He put in your hand.

The entire warfare and controversy over prosperity is to stop God from feelings of pleasure and feeling good about creating humans. You are not the only target. This whole battle does not revolve around you and your family. The controversy is between satan and God. You are only caught in the crossfire.

Your Seed is the only proof you are expecting something in return. The only evidence that a farmer is looking for a Harvest is when you see him sowing his Seed. Your Seed is the proof you are expecting.

Your words are not the proof. You can talk about many things and still not really be expecting a Harvest.

Now, *expectation is only possible when a Seed has been planted.*

When you withhold from God, it is impossible for your faith to work and expectation to occur. So, when God speaks to your heart to sow a Seed, you cannot even begin to expect a Harvest until you have obeyed His instruction. Your obedience in sowing immediately positions you to be able *to expect.*

Now, your sowing does not create expectation.

It makes it *possible for you* to expect.

You see, many people sow but they have not been taught the Principle of Seed-Faith — that *you should expect something in return.* So, millions give to churches and never see a huge return on their Seed. They give to pay the bills of the church. They give because of guilt over withholding after all the blessings they have experienced. They give because a pastor meets with them privately and insists on them making "a donation to the cause." They give for many reasons.

Few really sow their Seed to produce a Harvest.

Few sow with *expectation of a real return* from God.

How do you know that most do not expect a return? *They become angry over sowing.* If you believed something was coming back to you a hundred times — *you would be more excited in that moment than any other time of your life.*

Example: Have you ever received a sweepstakes letter in the mail that you have "won a million dollars?" Of course, you have. Now, when you are young and inexperienced, you get very excited. You tear the envelope open. You can just imagine yourself with a yacht, a beautiful Rolls Royce, and a vacation to Spain. What is happening? *Expectation excites you,* it energizes you, it creates a flurry of enthusiasm around you.

Expectation.

After you tear the envelope open, you suddenly realize there was part of the letter you could not see when it was closed. The part that says, "You *could be* one of those who win a million dollars." After you open the letter, you realize that they did not really promise that you had won it. But, *you may have been* one of the winners. Your expectation wanes and dies.

And withers. You make a telephone call and realize that you were not really one of the winners. Expectations dies. Disappointment sets in.

Any disappointment you are experiencing today reveals your lack of expectation of a Harvest.

So, watch and sense the atmosphere that fills a church when an offering is being received. If there is expectation of a Harvest, *joy will fill that house.*

If expectation is present, joy is present.

Joy is the proof of expectation.

Depression and disappointment are evidences of the presence of fear. The fear of loss. The fear of less.

Expectation is an impossibility until you sow a Seed.

You can have a need and *still not expect* an answer.

You can have a great dream and *still not expect it* to come to pass.

Expectation is produced by obedience.

Obedience is the proof of faith.

Faith is confidence in God.

Peter declared that he had given up everything to follow Christ. What was the reaction of Jesus? Well, He did not commend him for discipleship. He did not commend him for his willingness to suffer. He did not brag on him for being a martyr. Jesus looked at him and promised that he would get everything back that he gave up, *one hundred times over* (Mark 10:28-30).

Jesus constantly promoted expectation.

When the woman at the well of Samaria listened to Him, He promised her water that she would never thirst again. When the weary came to Him, He said, "I will give you rest." When the sinful approached Him with humility and confession, He promised them that they were forgiven.

Jesus always responded to those with great expectation. When the blind man cried out and was instructed to be silent by the crowds, Jesus reacted. Many were blind. But one had great expectations of Jesus.

Jesus healed him.

Impossible things happen to those who expect them to happen. "For verily I say unto you, that whosoever shall say unto this mountain, Be thou removed, and be thou cast into the sea; and shall not doubt in his heart, but shall believe that those things which he saith shall come to pass; he shall have whatsoever he saith" (Mark 11:23).

Anything good is going to find you.

Anything from God is going to *search you out.*

Anything excellent is going to *become obvious to you.*

That's the principle of Seed-Faith.

You have been given something by God that has a future. When you discover your Seed, wrap your faith around it with great expectation. This will empower you to produce the financial Harvest you have desired for your lifetime.

∼ 1 Kings 17:12,15 ∼

"And she said, As the Lord thy God liveth, I have not a cake, but an handful of meal in a barrel, and a little oil in a cruse: and behold, I am gathering two sticks, that I may go in and dress it for me and my son, that we may eat it, and die...And she went and did according to the saying of Elijah: and she and he, and her house, did eat many days."

⁓ 28 ⁓

Many Are Too Proud To Even Admit That They Need A Harvest.

Humility Is The Golden Key To Receiving.

Your needs do not attract God. Your *recognition* of your need attracts God. Every blind man did not receive the attention of God. Blind men who *wanted to see* attracted Jesus.

Poor widows did not receive all the miracles. A poor widow who *admitted she needed a miracle* received it (1 Kings 17).

Pride is a thief.

Arrogance will shut the door on your Harvest.

Many become poor trying to appear rich. I have known people who were three months late on their house payments, lost their car, but still they're telling everybody around them, "Things are going great."

Your miracle will not begin until you recognize that you need one.

We try so hard to impress each other. It almost becomes ridiculous. A few weeks back, I looked around the first class cabin I was riding in. One man sat there with a big smile on his face. He had a $40 briefcase that looked tattered. Holes in his clothes and shoes. But, he was going "first class." Something in me wanted to say, "If you would sit six feet further back, you could buy new clothes and a briefcase with the difference in the air fare!"

Pride disconnects us from right people. Pride is a horrible tragic and poisonous thing. It's deceptive. A young couple buying a house they cannot even afford shows pride. Oh, I have had the poison of pride in my own life so many times. There have been times that I needed a financial miracle, but I was ashamed to discuss it. I refused to tell a pastor or even my partners, because I believed in "prosperity." If I had admitted I needed a miracle Harvest, they would wonder "where's your prosperity that you have been teaching all this time?"

Remember the Pharisee who announced to God that he was glad he was not like the other man? But, across the synagogue was a publican kneeling before Him, pounding his chest and crying out for mercy? Pharisees were too proud to admit they needed a Savior.

Zacchaeus was not too proud. He climbed up in the tree to see Jesus. Oh, admit when you need a Harvest! Face your financial difficulties today. You do not have to complain, or beg, or act like a "victim" to get a miracle. But, you must admit to God, to yourself, and to intercessors assigned to stand with you that you truly need a financial miracle.

Admit that you need a financial advisor. Admit that you have withheld the tithe and the offerings when you have made this mistake.

Several years ago, I experienced the greatest financial crisis of my life. It happened suddenly. For a good while, my songs were sung everywhere. My royalty checks were incredible. Several hundred thousand dollars came into my hands quickly. I gave expensive gifts to my family, my friends, and my staff.

I took all my friends on vacations. I had more money than I had ever had in my lifetime.

Suddenly, a crisis came. I'll spare you the details, but I will simply say that I was suddenly in debt several hundred thousand dollars. As I said before, I could not even afford to pay $1,500 to a close friend, my CPA, to get a financial statement from him. (I was going to use this statement to get a loan from the bank.) Now, he had been a friend for many years. But, he refused to even do work for me and get me my financial statement so that I could get a loan!

I felt like a hypocrite. Here I was traveling and ministering about the Laws of Blessing. I had been swimming in the River of Plenty. Suddenly, it dried up. I was washed up on the Shore of Nothing.

My miracle began when I went into the presence of God and admitted that I needed supernatural intervention. I did not have the financial knowledge to turn it around. I did not have a wealthy board to stand with me. My family did not have any money. My partners were sowing everything they could.

The moment I cried out to God to show me a plan that would bring me out of trouble, the Holy Spirit began to walk me into my miracle. It didn't happen until I confessed my need.

Prayerlessness is proof you do not really believe God can help you.

Go to the Secret Place. Get alone with Him today. Confess everything you believe you should open up before Him. Do not be fearful. Do not be timid. Do not be protective of yourself. Confess everything.

You will then have taken the golden step toward supernatural supply.

≫ 2 Chronicles 20:20 ≪

"Believe in the Lord your God, so shall ye be established; believe His prophets, so shall ye prosper."

∾ 29 ∾

SOME REBEL AGAINST AN INSTRUCTION FROM A FINANCIAL DELIVERER GOD HAS ANOINTED TO UNLOCK THEIR FAITH DURING THEIR TIME OF CRISIS.

You Are Not Forgotten By God. Ever.

Nobody loves you more than the Person who created you. Your fears are known by Him. Your tears matter to Him. When you are hurting, He is bringing answers toward you. Every moment of your life God schedules miracles like currents of blessing into your life.

Every prison will have a door.

Every river will have a bridge.

Every mountain will have a tunnel.

But, you must find it. Look for it. Listen for it. Search for it. Believe that it exists. "There hath no temptation taken you but such as is common to man: but God is faithful, who will not suffer you to be tempted above that ye are able; but will with the temptation also make a way to escape, that ye may be able to bear it" (1 Corinthians 10:13).

You must pursue those God is using to fuel your faith. There are wonderful men and women of God who carry financial anointings. They can unlock your faith. It may involve a four-hour drive to their crusade. *But it is very important that you honor and treasure and pursue their mantle.* Listen to their tapes. Read their books. Listen to their heart.

They have tasted failure. *They know how to get out of trouble.* They know what sleepless nights are like. They have fought the demons of fear and uncertainty.

That's why they are qualified to mentor you.

Some will never taste their financial Harvest because they are sitting under leaders *who fuel their doubts* and unbelief. They listen to *relatives* who continuously discuss the economic problems on the earth, hard times and how difficult life is.

The voices you keep listening to are the voices you will eventually believe.

Ten spies infected millions of the Israelites with their unbelief and doubt. When they talked about the giants, the people forgot about the grapes of blessing.

What you talk about increases.

What you think about becomes larger.

Your mind and your mouth are magnifiers of anything you want to *grow*.

Two spies came back with faith, victory and the ability to overcome giants. Their names were Joshua and Caleb. They had been with God. They had seen the giants, but were not afraid. They had seen the grapes and decided to become champions. They had experienced too many days in the wilderness to be satisfied with failure.

They became the champions of faith. Joshua became the leader after the death of Moses. Caleb became known for "taking his mountain." Oh, the rewards of faith are sweet. The taste of victory stays in your mouth so long!

You must discern the Joshuas and Calebs around you. Find the faith food. Listen for faith talk. Sit under it and listen and absorb. *Something within you will grow.*

I receive much inspiration from the story of Elijah and the widow in 1 Kings 17. I never tire of this incredible Well of Wisdom. She was hurting. Devastated. Starving. She was one meal from death.

That's when a man of faith was sent into her life.

He did not criticize her, coddle her, or sympathize with her. He knew *how* to get her *out of trouble.*

She had to listen to him. She had to discern that he was a man of God. She had to be willing to follow his instructions, regardless of how ridiculous and illogical they appeared to her *natural* mind.

A man of God often holds the Golden Key to your financial deliverance. If you respect that anointing, the chains will fall off. Blindness will disappear. Your eyes will behold the golden path to blessing. If you become critical, resentful, and rebellious, you will forfeit the most remarkable season of miracles God has ever scheduled into your life.

Nobody can discern a man of God for you. You must do it yourself.

Nobody can force you to obey a man of God. Your

heart must be soft and broken before God enough to follow.

You may only receive one opportunity to obey the instruction that brings your deliverance. (Nabal only received one opportunity to feed and bless the army of David.)

You must recognize greatness when you are in the presence of it. It will not always demand attention. Jesus visited many places where He was undiscerned, undetected and unrecognized. His own family did not recognize His mantle, His Assignment, and that He was the Son of God. He did come unto His own and His own received Him not.

You may have to find the man of God before he blesses you. You see, he is *not* needing *you.* You are needing him.

Read the incredible story of Saul and his servant, who had lost their donkeys. They were so disturbed until the servant *remembered that a man of God* lived in the area. He knew the power of an offering. They both made the decision to find the Prophet Samuel. The rest of the story is absolutely incredible. When they came into the presence of Samuel, the anointing from Samuel began to flow toward them. (See 1 Samuel 9:3-10:10.)

They had brought their Seed.

They brought an offering.

They believed he was a man of God.

That encounter with Samuel catapulted Saul into the kingship of Israel.

Somewhere, there is a man of God with the golden key to your house of treasure. Your responsibility is to discern it, find him, and *obey* the instruction.

Several years ago, my assistant listened to me share the miracle of the "Covenant of Blessing," the sowing of the $58 Seed. (My first encounter was in Washington, DC, when the Holy Spirit spoke to me to plant a $58 Seed to represent the 58 kinds of miracles I had found in Scripture. It launched an incredible parade of miracles into my personal life. I have told about this in hundreds of places.)

Now, my assistant was a good young man who loved God. But, something happened as he listened to me tell the story. I instructed him and others in that service to give their Seed "an Assignment." "Write on the check where you want to experience the Harvest in your own personal life," I instructed.

He wrote his $58 Seed, and then wrote on his check, "better family relations." Here is what happened following that Seed:

1. His mother came to Christ within 14 days.
2. His two sisters came to Christ within 14 days.
3. His daughter came to Christ within 14 days.
4. He got to spend a week with two of his other daughters that he had not even seen in five years.
5. He was able to have a meal and afternoon with his entire family — this had not happened in the previous 15 years.
6. His 86-year-old father came to Christ within 90 days.
7. His oldest sister, who had run away from home 48 years prior, was located and came back home for a family reunion. (Nobody had seen nor heard from her for 48 long

years. She was considered dead.)

Every one of these miracles happened within 90 days of his sowing his Seed of $58.

Why? *He followed the instruction of a man of God.* Almost everywhere I go, I ask those who need miracles to plant a Seed. A specific Seed. Usually, I ask them to plant a Seed of $58 (sometimes it is more, depending on the instructions of the Holy Spirit). The miracles are incredible. I get letters from everywhere relating the supernatural intervention of God *following their acts of obedience.*

A woman in Knoxville, Tennessee, approached me with a tall husband by her side. "Remember that $58 Seed?" she asked.

"Yes."

"This is him! He was away from Christ and within a few days after my Seed, he came with me to church and gave his heart to God."

Those God sends may not be packaged like you anticipated. John the Baptist had an appearance many could not tolerate. But, God was with him. God's best gifts do not always arrive in silk. He often uses burlap bags to package his best prizes. Men do look on the outward appearance, while God looks on the heart.

Those God sends into your life may have harsh or uncomfortable personalities. If you could have heard Isaiah or Ezekiel, you might be shocked at some of the strong language that poured from their lips.

Those God sends with a special challenge to your faith may not appear socially fit. God often uses foolish things to confound the wise. You will not discern them through the hearing of the ear or the seeing of the eye.

You will discern them by the Spirit of God within you.

"Believe in the Lord your God, so shall ye be established; believe his prophets, so shall ye prosper" (2 Chronicles 20:20).

When you begin to acknowledge the Word of the Lord coming from proven and established servants of God, the flow of miracles will multiply and increase toward you.

2 Corinthians 9:6

"He which soweth sparingly shall reap also sparingly; and he which soweth bountifully shall reap also bountifully."

∾ 30 ∾

Many Refuse To Sow Proportionate To The Harvest They Desire.

────◆────

The Size Of Your Seed Determines The Size Of Your Harvest.

The Apostle Paul made this clear, "He which soweth sparingly shall reap also sparingly; and he which soweth bountifully shall reap also bountifully" (2 Corinthians 9:6).

I will never forget an experience in the Northeast. A large lady moved toward me after the service.

"I'm believing God to make me a millionaire. And, I believe it will happen within 12 months. Here's my Seed to make it happen." She thrust something into my hand. I looked at her and said, "I am believing God with you."

After she walked away, I opened my hand. It was a crumpled dollar bill. *A dollar bill.*

Now there is nothing wrong with sowing a small Seed. *Everything must have a beginning point.* Jesus commended the woman who gave a small offering — *because it was all she had.* He said that she gave more than anyone else present that day.

But, Jesus did *not* say that her small offering was necessarily going to make her a *millionaire.* You see, *your Seed must be comparable to the Harvest you are sowing toward.*

You cannot plant a Chevrolet Seed and produce a Rolls Royce Harvest. This was what Paul was teaching. If you sow small, you will still reap. But, it will not be a large Harvest. *It will be proportionate to your Seed.*

Millions have not grasped this. They continue to roll up dollar bills, drop them in the offering plate, and hope no one watches. Yet, they are writing their prayer requests as if they are expecting Cadillacs, yachts, and million dollar homes.

You can *begin* with a small Seed. When God begins to bless that small Seed, *you must increase the size of the Seed if you want the Harvest to increase.*

Let me give you an example. If you come to me and say, "Mike, I really need a house. My family is growing. I have three children. Right now, my wife and three children are living in a small two bedroom apartment. It is almost unbearable. We do not even have a refrigerator, or a car. What should I do?"

First, I will not tell you to plant a $5.00 Seed toward your $100,000 home you are wanting. I would encourage you to work with your various levels of faith in front of you. *A step at a time.*

Obviously, you have not been operating with great faith or you would not be in this kind of situation.

Your faith has been low.

Your Seeds have not been planted.

Or, patience is a needed ingredient for this season.

"What is the best Seed you can sow at this time? What kind of faith is operating in you today?" I ask.

"Oh, I have $50 that I want to plant," you answer.

I would reply, "Wonderful. Now, let's focus this Seed for an automobile comparable to this Seed. Do not ask for a $20,000 automobile from a $50 Seed. That is four times the promised hundredfold of Mark 10:28-30. Obviously, you're not accustomed to planting Seed, using your faith, or even working with the laws of patience and expectation.

Ask God for something you cannot doubt. Then, plant a Seed comparable to the Harvest you have pure faith toward. You must separate your wishes from your faith. You must separate your fantasies from your faith.

Now, many do not understand the *Principle of Progress.* Line upon line. Precept upon precept. Here a little and there a little. There is a season of "growing up" in your Christian life.

It is the same principle in the financial arena of your life. Why is this so important? When you sow a $2.00 Seed toward something that is out of balance, you will become disappointed, discouraged and disillusioned. You will become angry at God. You will say, "I planted a Seed and this did not multiply!"

Maybe it is multiplying! Maybe, the $100 bill you have in your purse was produced by the $2.00 Seed. But, you're not noticing it because you wanted a $20,000 Harvest.

You must learn to move from glory to glory.

I told about an incredible miracle in my life one night. I was sitting in a beautiful Mustang convertible. Teal bottom and white top. Gorgeous. It had "fun" written all over the car!

"I just bought this car this week," my friend explained. "However, I decided that I want a jeep instead. Do you think you might want to buy this car from me?"

"I think I may!" was my reply.

The next day, we pulled up at a service station. After he filled the tank, he went inside to pay the bill. I began to pray in the Spirit. Suddenly, I began to feel a *faith rise up in me* for him to sow this as a Seed into my life. Now, that sounds a little crazy. But, I began to pray intensely. When he got back in the car, he looked at me. He cocked his head sideways and said, "You really like this car?"

"I love this car," I gushed.

"Your ministry has so affected and blessed me, I have been wondering what I could do to bless you." He handed me the keys with a smile. The car was mine. Free. An incredible gift that will stay in my heart forever.

So, when I was in a crusade later, I shared this story. I told everyone that I was going to pray that the *mantle of favor* would come upon their life. I explained that *one day of favor was worth a thousand days of labor.* When God wants to bless you, He puts somebody close to you who cares about your life and needs.

A young man approached me after church a little disgruntled. Agitated. Frustrated.

"I did that already and it did not work," he explained. "I planted a Seed several months ago and I have never had a car given to me. I need transportation. Why didn't it work for me?"

"Have you ever *planted* a car in the life of someone else?" I asked.

"No, I have not," was his hesitant and reluctant reply.

"I have. That's why my faith worked for me. I had already planted a car and I had every right and ability to expect one to be *given back to me*," I explained.

You cannot expect toward your life what you have not faithed away from your life.

You will only have the faith to call in toward your life *something that you have sowed out.*

Now, there are wonderful moments of mercy and grace where God will let something that you have been given — money, a piece of jewelry or whatever — and He will use that as a picture of your faith for a different kind of Harvest. I've seen that happen many many times. But, your faith works *the most, the strongest,* when you have planted a Seed comparable to the Harvest you would desire.

When you are willing to work with the different levels of your faith and sow Seed proportionately, you will be amazed at the changes that will happen in your financial prosperity.

❧ Ephesians 4:30 ❧

"And grieve not the Holy Spirit of God,
whereby ye are sealed unto the day of
redemption."

≈ 31 ≈

Millions Do Not Instantly Obey The Holy Spirit Without Negotiation.

The Holy Spirit Will Not Argue With You.

He is the gift of the Father to those who obey Him. He will woo you. He will tug on your heart. He is gentle, kind and long-suffering.

But, *He will not enter into a debate with you.* He despises strife, confusion and struggle. "And the servant of the Lord must not strive; but be gentle unto all men" (2 Timothy 2:24).

He will move away from your attacks and quarrelsome spirit. "But foolish and unlearned questions avoid, knowing that they do gender strifes." (2 Timothy 2:23).

Do not argue with the *Source of your supply.* Stop looking for reasons to avoid sowing. Honor His integrity. He is not unfair. He is not unjust. When He whispers to your heart to take a step of faith, leap forward. Run toward your Harvest.

"Well, I don't want to simply plant out of an emotional feeling!" one minister friend of mine explained.

"Everything you do is emotional," I replied.

"When you drag a moment of faith through the sewage of logic, *you destroy its impact and influence.* Be swift to obey His voice."

I experienced an unusual miracle in my life when I was about 23 years old. I had been on the evangelistic field two or three years. My first year as an evangelist brought me $2,263 income. (One month my entire income was $35. Another month it was $90. I lived in a house that my father had purchased for $150. The entire house!)

Eventually, I had enough money saved to buy a suit and some clothes. It had taken a good while, but I finally saved up $200. I had two $100 bills inside my wallet. I was rather proud but thankful for it. I felt secure. I was anxious to get to a store to buy some clothes.

A young evangelist friend of mine was preaching in a local church. So, I decided to hear him. While he was speaking, I felt the inner tug of the Holy Spirit to plant the $200 into his ministry. I explained to the Lord that my plans were to purchase clothes, so I could look good for His work. The longer he ministered, the more miserable I felt. A heaviness was in me. I thought of every reason to keep the $200. Inside, I began to *negotiate* with the Holy Spirit. I really did not have a desire to plant any Seed whatsoever. But I knew His voice.

Somewhere, during some service of a man of God the Holy Spirit is going to raise your level of desire to *please Him.* You may not have a lot of joy during the sowing. You may even experience inner conflict and mind confusion, but *something in you will become strong* and intense that your desire to please Him will overwhelm your logic, your fears and your greed.

It is that miracle moment when your desire to obey Him becomes so powerful that you *open the windows of heaven toward your life.*

After the service, I went to him and handed him the $200. He was thrilled. I was rather saddened but tried to hide it. It was my clothes money.

Seven days later, I was laying in bed at midnight. The telephone rang.

"Brother Mike Murdock?"

"Yes?"

"You don't really know me. My husband and I were in your services a year ago here in Memphis. My son died four weeks ago, and God told my husband and I to start treating you like our boy. God told us to buy you some clothes. Are you coming through Memphis any time soon?" *What do you think!* I didn't care if I had to go through Australia and Russia to get to Memphis, I was going to arrive in Memphis... very soon.

When I got off the plane, she took me to the nicest men's store in Memphis, Tennessee. She bought me four suits, shirts and shoes. Six months later, they did it again. Six months later, they did it again. Six months later, they did it again. And again. Again. And again.

Later, I went to hear a friend of mine in Houston at his church on a Sunday night. Halfway through his sermon, he stopped. He pointed back to me on the back row and said, "It is so good to have Mike Murdock here tonight. The Holy Spirit just spoke to me to stop the service and receive him *an offering to buy him some clothes.*" I was stunned.

On a Wednesday night, I drove across town to another church. I had never met this pastor before.

Halfway through his Bible study, he looked back and noticed me on the back seat.

"I see Mike Murdock here tonight. Brother, you and I have never met before, but I have seen you in various conferences. It is wonderful to have you. The Holy Spirit just spoke to my heart to stop the service and receive you an offering *to buy you some clothes.*"

I was in Louisville, Kentucky, and my pastor friend said, "What are you doing tomorrow morning?"

"What do *you want to do?*" I replied.

"The Holy Spirit spoke to my heart *to buy you some clothes,*" he replied.

I was sitting next to a minister friend of mine in Illinois. He leaned over to me and whispers in church, "When are you leaving tomorrow?"

"Why?" I asked.

"I felt the Lord wanted me to *buy you a Breoni suit tomorrow.*" (The next day he purchased it for me. Though he got it wholesale, the retail price on it was $3,220!)

One of my closest friends, Nancy Harmon, called me to her house. I walked in and there were clothes from one end of the room to the other. "The Lord told me *to buy you some clothes,*" she said.

> **What You Are Willing To Walk Away From Determines What God Will Bring To You.**

You see, I had walked way from my clothes money. Now, God was supernaturally talking to people about replacing my clothes money by purchasing clothes for me.

What You Are Willing To Walk Away From Determines What God Will Bring To You.

Please, never argue with the

Source of every miracle you are desiring. *When He Talks To You About A Seed, He Has A Harvest On His Mind.*

You see, He knew *the future* He was planning. So He gave me faith to plant the Seed *that would create my desired future.* He gave me the desire, the Seed and the soil where it would grow the quickest.

When God Talks To You About Sowing A Seed He Has A Harvest On His Mind.

You can *grieve* the Holy Spirit through debating.

You can cause Him to *withdraw* from you when you negotiate and *move away from faith.*

Faith attracts Him. Faith excites Him. Expectation is His pleasure. *Do not rob Him of that moment of obedience.*

Delayed obedience can become disobedience.

Millions have lost a thousand Harvests because they became intellectual, negotiative, and argumentative when the Holy Spirit began to whisper an instruction to their heart.

I was in Jacksonville, Florida, a few days ago. The secretary of the pastor came to me weeping. Her husband was by her side.

"Here is the best Seed God has told us to sow. Please take it." It was her wedding rings, the most precious treasure she had. *(When you plant a Seed that you can feel, God will feel too. You must plant something significant to you before it becomes significant to God.)*

That was Monday night.

Five days later, Friday night, she stood at a special School of the Holy Spirit with incredible joy on her countenance and gave her testimony. Somebody who knew nothing of her sacrificial Seed of all of her rings had decided to bless her. They become a Boaz to her. *They gave her a ring worth 100 times the cost of her own rings.*

"And Jesus answered and said, Verily I say unto you, there is no man that hath left house, or brethren, or sisters, or father, or mother, or wife, or children, or lands, for my sake, and the gospel's, But he shall receive an hundredfold now in this time, houses, and brethren, and sisters, and mothers, and children, and lands, with persecutions; and in the world to come eternal life" (Mark 10:28-30).

God is *not a man* that He should lie.

He wants to be *believed.*

Nobody can use your faith for you.

Nobody can dream bigger for you.

Nobody can plant the Seed for you.

Nobody. Not your mother, nor father, nor boss, nor child.

Every man will give an account of himself to God.

Sometimes, I picture this scenario. Everybody is approaching the Throne of Accountability. They want answers to questions. They want God to explain *why they were poor.* He will ask the same question.

"Why were you poor when I promised you one hundredfold return for anything you would plant in My work? I told you if you would obey My principles, be diligent and expect Me to do what I promised, I would open the windows of heaven and pour you out a blessing that you could not contain. I, too, want to know why you decided to disregard my instructions and remain without the financial Harvest?"

That might be the *Weeping Night of Eternity* when everybody recognizes that the principles were accessible, available and usable — just ignored.

Now, you can begin your own journey to prosperity. Be willing to take it a step at a time. Do not rush it. Be careful to *obey* His voice. *Review* this book carefully. Bring it with you into the *Secret Place* of prayer. Talk to the Holy Spirit and ask Him *every single step* you should take at this time. Bring your stack of bills and credit cards and place them on top of this book. Anoint them, and *invite the supernatural intervention of God* to break the financial poverty and spirit of lack that has affected and influenced your life.

Ask Him to give you a hatred of poverty and a love and desire for supernatural provision. *Discuss your dreams and financial goals in detail with Him.* Believe that He will send a Boaz into your life to bless you in many ways.

When He talks to your heart about planting a Seed into His work, don't hesitate. Don't negotiate. And, don't manipulate. The Holy Spirit honors integrity where He finds it.

Confess any sin. Admit if you have withheld the tithes and the offerings He asked. Repent with humility, integrity and expectation of a change in your life.

You will see the changes come sooner than you dreamed.

TODAY IS THE POOREST YOU WILL EVER BE THE REST OF YOUR LIFE.

Let's pray:

"Father, I've opened my heart, and sowed the revelation that changed my life forever. Now, use this Seed to grow an Uncommon Harvest. Oh, bless the obedient, the willing and the hungry. In Jesus' name. Amen."

"An Uncommon Harvest Will Always Require An Uncommon Seed."

MIKE MURDOCK

DECISION

Will You Accept Jesus As Your Personal Savior Today?

The Bible says, "That if thou shalt confess with thy mouth the Lord Jesus, and shalt believe in thine heart that God hath raised Him from the dead, thou shalt be saved" (Rom. 10:9).

Pray this prayer from your heart today!

"Dear Jesus, I believe that You died for me and rose again on the third day. I confess I am a sinner...I need Your love and forgiveness... Come into my heart. Forgive my sins. I receive Your eternal life. Confirm Your love by giving me peace, joy and supernatural love for others. Amen."

Clip and Mail

DR. MIKE MURDOCK

is in tremendous demand as one of the most dynamic speakers in America today.

More than 15,000 audiences in 39 countries have attended his meetings and seminars. Hundreds of invitations come to him from churches, colleges and business corporations. He is a noted author of over 160 books, including the best sellers, *"The Leadership Secrets of Jesus"* and *"Secrets of the Richest Man Who Ever Lived."* Thousands view his weekly television program, *"Wisdom Keys with Mike Murdock."* Many attend his Schools of Wisdom that he hosts in major cities of America.

☐ Yes, Mike! I made a decision to accept Christ as my personal Savior today. Please send me my free gift of your book, *"31 Keys to a New Beginning"* to help me with my new life in Christ. *(B-48)*

NAME   BIRTHDAY

ADDRESS

CITY   STATE   ZIP

PHONE   E-MAIL   *B-82*

Mail form to:
The Wisdom Center • *4051 Denton Highway* • *Denton, TX 76117*
Phone: 1-888-WISDOM-1 (1-817-759-0300)
*Website: **www.TheWisdomCenter.TV***

THE MAN
DR. MIKE MURDOCK

1 Has embraced his Assignment to Pursue...Proclaim...and Publish the Wisdom of God to help people achieve their dreams and goals.

2 Began full-time evangelism at the age of 19, which has continued since 1966.

3 Has traveled and spoken to more than 15,000 audiences in 39 countries, including East and West Africa, the Orient, and Europe.

4 Noted author of 160 books, including best sellers, "Wisdom For Winning,," "Dream Seeds" and "The Double Diamond Principle."

5 Created the popular "Topical Bible" series for Businessmen, Mothers, Fathers, Teenagers; "The One-Minute Pocket Bible" series, and "The Uncommon Life" series.

6 Has composed more than 5,700 songs such as "I Am Blessed," "You Can Make It," "God Rides On Wings Of Love" and "Jesus Just The Mention Of Your Name," recorded by many gospel artists.

7 Is the Founder of The Wisdom Center, in Fort Worth, Texas.

8 Has a weekly television program called "Wisdom Keys With Mike Murdock."

9 Has appeared often on TBN, CBN, BET and other television network programs.

10 Is a Founding Trustee on the Board of International Charismatic Bible Ministries with Oral Roberts.

11 Has had more than 3,500 accept the call into full-time ministry under his ministry.

THE
MINISTRY

1 Wisdom Books & Literature Over 160 best-selling Wisdom Books and 70 Teaching Tape Series..

2 Church Crusades - Multitudes are ministered to in crusades and seminars throughout America in "The Uncommon Wisdom Conferences." Known as a man who loves pastors, he has focused on church crusades for 36 years.

3 Music Ministry - Millions have been blessed by the anointed songwriting and singing of Mike Murdock, who has made over 15 music albums and CDs available.

4 Television - "Wisdom Keys With Mike Murdock," a nationally-syndicated weekly television program.

5 The Wisdom Center - The Ministry Offices where Dr. Murdock holds an annual School of Wisdom for those desiring The Uncommon Life.

6 Schools of the Holy Spirit - Mike Murdock hosts Schools of The Holy Spirit in many churches to mentor believers on the Person and companionship of The Holy Spirit.

7 Schools of Wisdom - In 12 major cities Mike Murdock hosts Saturday Schools of Wisdom for those who want personalized and advanced training for achieving "The Uncommon Dream."

8 Missionary Ministry - Dr. Murdock's overseas outreaches to 39 countries have included crusades in East and West Africa, South America and Europe.

Your Letter Is Very Important to Me

Y ou are a special person to me, and I believe that you are special to God. I want to assist you in any way possible. Write me when you need an intercessor to pray for you. When you write, my staff and I will pray over your letter. I will write you back.

Mike, please enter into the prayer of agreement with me for the following needs:
(Please Print)

_____

_____

_____

_____

_____

_____

_____

_____

_____

_____

_____

_____

_____

Mail to:
The Wisdom Center • *4051 Denton Highway* •*Denton, TX 76117*
Phone: 1-888-WISDOM-1 (1-817-759-0300)
Website: ***www.TheWisdomCenter.TV***

ORDER FORM THE WISDOM CENTER

(All books paperback unless indicated otherwise.)

Qty	Code	Book Title	USA	Total
	B-01	Wisdom for Winning	$10	
	B-02	Five Steps Out of Depression	$ 3	
	B-03	The Sex Trap	$ 5	
	B-04	Ten Lies Many People Believe About Money	$ 5	
	B-05	Finding Your Purpose in Life	$ 3	
	B-06	Creating Tomorrow Through Seed-Faith	$ 5	
	B-07	Battle Techniques for War Weary Saints	$ 5	
	B-08	Enjoying the Winning Life	$ 3	
	B-09	Four Forces That Guarantee Career Success	$ 3	
	B-10	The Bridge Called Divorce	$ 5	
	B-11	Dream Seeds	$ 9	
	B-12	The Ministers Encyclopedia, Vol. 1	$30	
	B-13	Seeds of Wisdom on Dreams And Goals, Vol. 1	$ 3	
	B-14	Seeds of Wisdom on Relationships, Vol. 2	$ 3	
	B-15	Seeds of Wisdom on Miracles, Vol. 3	$ 3	
	B-16	Seeds of Wisdom on Seed-Faith, Vol. 4	$ 3	
	B-17	Seeds of Wisdom on Overcoming, Vol. 5	$ 3	
	B-18	Seeds of Wisdom on Habits, Vol. 6	$ 3	
	B-19	Seeds of Wisdom on Warfare, Vol. 7	$ 3	
	B-20	Seeds of Wisdom on Obedience, Vol. 8	$ 3	
	B-21	Seeds of Wisdom on Adversity, Vol. 9	$ 3	
	B-22	Seeds of Wisdom on Prosperity, Vol. 10	$ 3	
	B-23	Seeds of Wisdom on Prayer, Vol. 11	$ 3	
	B-24	Seeds of Wisdom on Faith-Talk, Vol. 12	$ 3	
	B-25	7 Kinds of People You Cannot Help	$ 5	
	B-26	The God Book	$10	
	B-27	The Jesus Book	$10	
	B-28	The Blessing Bible	$10	
	B-29	The Survival Bible	$10	
	B-30	The Teen's Topical Bible	$10	
	B-31	Seeds of Wisdom Topical Bible	$10	
	B-32	The Minister's Topical Bible	$10	
	B-33	The Businessman's Topical Bible	$10	
	B-34	The Grandparent's Topical Bible	$10	
	B-35	The Father's Topical Bible	$10	
	B-36	The Mother's Topical Bible	$10	
	B-37	The New Convert's Bible	$10	
	B-38	The Widow's Topical Bible	$10	
	B-39	The Double Diamond Principle	$ 9	
	B-40	Wisdom for Crisis Times	$ 9	
	B-41	The Gift of Wisdom, Vol. 1	$10	
	B-42	One-Minute Businessman's Devotional	$12	
	B-43	One-Minute Businesswoman's Devotional	$12	
	B-44	31 Secrets for Career Success	$10	
	B-45	101 Wisdom Keys	$ 5	
	B-46	31 Facts About Wisdom	$ 5	
	B-47	The Covenant of The Fifty-Eight Blessings	$ 8	
	B-48	31 Keys to a New Beginning	$ 5	
	B-49	The Proverbs 31 Woman	$ 7	
	B-50	One-Minute Pocket Bible for Achievers	$ 5	
	B-51	One-Minute Pocket Bible for Fathers	$ 5	
	B-52	One-Minute Pocket Bible for Mothers	$ 5	
	B-53	One-Minute Pocket Bible for Teenagers	$ 5	
	B-54	31 Greatest Chapters In The Bible	$10	
	B-55	20 Keys to a Happier Marriage	$ 7	
	B-56	How to Turn Mistakes into Miracles	$ 5	

QTY	CODE	BOOK TITLE	USA	TOTAL
	B-57	31 SECRETS OF AN UNFORGETTABLE WOMAN	$ 9	
	B-58	THE MENTOR'S MANNA ON ATTITUDE	$ 3	
	B-59	THE MAKING OF A CHAMPION	$10	
	B-60	ONE-MINUTE POCKET BIBLE FOR MEN	$ 5	
	B-61	ONE-MINUTE POCKET BIBLE FOR WOMEN	$ 5	
	B-62	ONE-MINUTE POCKET BIBLE/BUS.PROFESSIONALS	$ 5	
	B-63	ONE-MINUTE POCKET BIBLE FOR TRUCKERS	$ 5	
	B-64	SEVEN OBSTACLES TO ABUNDANT SUCCESS	$ 3	
	B-65	BORN TO TASTE THE GRAPES	$ 3	
	B-66	GREED, GOLD AND GIVING	$ 3	
	B-67	GIFT OF WISDOM FOR CHAMPIONS	$10	
	B-68	GIFT OF WISDOM FOR ACHIEVERS	$10	
	B-69	WISDOM KEYS FOR A POWERFUL PRAYER LIFE	$ 3	
	B-70	GIFT OF WISDOM FOR MOTHERS	$10	
	B-71	WISDOM - GOD'S GOLDEN KEY TO SUCCESS	$ 7	
	B-72	THE DOUBLE DIAMOND DAILY DEVOTIONAL	$15	
	B-73	THE MENTOR'S MANNA ON ABILITIES	$ 3	
	B-74	THE ASSIGNMENT: DREAM/DESTINY, VOL. 1	$10	
	B-75	THE ASSIGNMENT: ANOINTING/ADVERSITY, VOL. 2	$10	
	B-76	THE MENTOR'S MANNA ON ASSIGNMENT	$ 3	
	B-77	THE GIFT OF WISDOM FOR FATHERS	$10	
	B-78	THE MENTOR'S MANNA ON THE SECRET PLACE	$ 3	
	B-79	THE MENTOR'S MANNA ON ACHIEVEMENT	$ 3	
	B-80	THE GREATEST SUCCESS HABIT ON EARTH	$ 3	
	B-81	THE MENTOR'S MANNA ON ADVERSITY	$ 3	
	B-82	31 REASONS PEOPLE DO NOT RECEIVE THEIR FINANCIAL HARVEST	$12	
	B-83	THE GIFT OF WISDOM FOR WIVES	$10	
	B-84	THE GIFT OF WISDOM FOR HUSBANDS	$10	
	B-85	THE GIFT OF WISDOM FOR TEENAGERS	$10	
	B-86	THE GIFT OF WISDOM FOR LEADERS	$10	
	B-87	THE GIFT OF WISDOM FOR GRADUATES	$10	
	B-88	THE GIFT OF WISDOM FOR BRIDES	$10	
	B-89	THE GIFT OF WISDOM FOR GROOMS	$10	
	B-90	THE GIFT OF WISDOM FOR MINISTERS	$10	
	B-91	THE LEADERSHIP SECRETS OF JESUS	$10	
	B-92	SECRETS OF THE JOURNEY, VOL. 1	$ 5	
	B-93	SECRETS OF THE JOURNEY, VOL. 2	$ 5	
	B-94	SECRETS OF THE JOURNEY, VOL. 3	$ 5	
	B-95	SECRETS OF THE JOURNEY, VOL. 4	$ 5	
	B-96	SECRETS OF THE JOURNEY, VOL. 5	$ 5	
	B-97	THE ASSIGNMENT: TRIALS/TRIUMPHS, VOL. 3	$10	
	B-98	THE ASSIGNMENT: PAIN/PASSION, VOL. 4	$10	
	B-99	SECRETS OF THE RICHEST MAN WHO EVER LIVED	$10	
	B-100	THE HOLY SPIRIT HANDBOOK, VOL. 1	$10	
	B-101	THE 3 MOST IMPORTANT THINGS IN YOUR LIFE	$10	
	B-102	SECRETS OF THE JOURNEY, VOL. 6	$ 5	
	B-103	SECRETS OF THE JOURNEY, VOL. 7	$ 5	
	B-104	7 KEYS TO 1000 TIMES MORE	$10	
	B-105	31 DAYS FOR SUCCEEDING ON YOUR JOB	$10	
	B-106	THE UNCOMMON LEADER	$10	
	B-107	THE UNCOMMON MINISTER, VOL. 1	$ 5	
	B-108	THE UNCOMMON MINISTER, VOL. 2	$ 5	
	B-109	THE UNCOMMON MINISTER, VOL. 3	$ 5	
	B-110	THE UNCOMMON MINISTER, VOL. 4	$ 5	
	B-111	THE UNCOMMON MINISTER, VOL. 5	$ 5	
	B-112	THE UNCOMMON MINISTER, VOL. 6	$ 5	
	B-113	THE UNCOMMON MINISTER, VOL. 7	$ 5	

Qty	Code	Book Title	USA	Total
	B-114	The Law of Recognition	$10	
	B-115	Seeds of Wisdom on the Secret Place, Vol. 13	$ 5	
	B-116	Seeds of Wisdom on the Holy Spirit, Vol. 14	$ 5	
	B-117	Seeds of Wisdom on the Word Of God, Vol. 15	$ 5	
	B-118	Seeds of Wisdom on Problem Solving, Vol. 16	$ 5	
	B-119	Seeds of Wisdom on Favor, Vol. 17	$ 5	
	B-120	Seeds of Wisdom on Healing, Vol. 18	$ 5	
	B-121	Seeds of Wisdom on Time-Management, Vol. 19	$ 5	
	B-122	Seeds of Wisdom on Your Assignment, Vol. 20	$ 5	
	B-123	Seeds of Wisdom on Financial Breakthrough, Vol. 21	$ 5	
	B-124	Seeds of Wisdom on Enemies, Vol. 22	$ 5	
	B-125	Seeds of Wisdom on Decision-Making, Vol. 23	$ 5	
	B-126	Seeds of Wisdom on Mentorship Vol. 24	$ 5	
	B-127	Seeds of Wisdom on Goal-Setting, Vol. 25	$ 5	
	B-128	Seeds of Wisdom on the Power of Words, Vol. 26	$ 5	
	B-129	The Secret of the Seed	$10	
	B-130	The Uncommon Millionaire, Vol. 1	$10	
	B-131	The Uncommon Father	$10	
	B-132	The Uncommon Mother	$10	
	B-133	The Uncommon Achiever	$10	
	B-134	The Uncommon Armorbearer	$10	
	B-135	The Uncommon Dream, Vol. 1	$10	

☐ CASH ☐ CHECK ☐ MONEY ORDER

☐ CREDIT CARD # ☐ VISA ☐ MC ☐ AMEX

EXPIRATION DATE ☐☐☐☐☐☐ *SORRY NO C.O.D.'s*

Signature _____

TOTAL PAGES 1, 2, 3	$
SHIPPING ADD 10%-USA/20%-OTHERS	$
CANADA CURRENCY DIFFERENCE ADD 20%	$
TOTAL ENCLOSED	$

PLEASE PRINT

Name _____

Address _____

City _____ State _____ Zip _____

Phone ( ) -

E-mail _____

Mail to: **The Wisdom Center** • 4051 Denton Highway • Fort Worth, TX 76117
1-888-WISDOM-1 (1-817-759-0300) • Website: **TheWisdomCenter.TV**

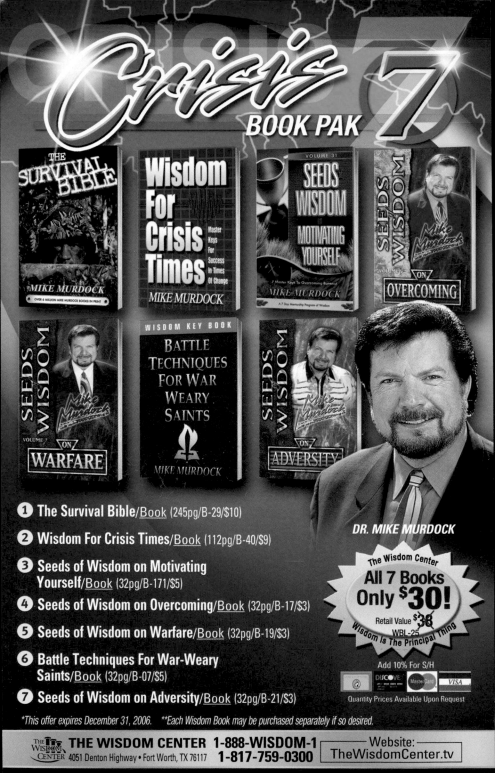

Crisis BOOK PAK 7

THE SURVIVAL BIBLE · MIKE MURDOCK · OVER 6 MILLION MIKE MURDOCK BOOKS IN PRINT

Wisdom For Crisis Times · Master Keys For Success In Times Of Change · MIKE MURDOCK

VOLUME 31 · **SEEDS WISDOM MOTIVATING YOURSELF** · MIKE MURDOCK

SEEDS WISDOM ON OVERCOMING

SEEDS WISDOM ON WARFARE · VOLUME 7

WISDOM KEY BOOK · **BATTLE TECHNIQUES FOR WAR WEARY SAINTS** · MIKE MURDOCK

SEEDS WISDOM ON ADVERSITY

① The Survival Bible/<u>Book</u> (245pg/B-29/$10)

② Wisdom For Crisis Times/<u>Book</u> (112pg/B-40/$9)

③ Seeds of Wisdom on Motivating Yourself/<u>Book</u> (32pg/B-171/$5)

④ Seeds of Wisdom on Overcoming/<u>Book</u> (32pg/B-17/$3)

⑤ Seeds of Wisdom on Warfare/<u>Book</u> (32pg/B-19/$3)

⑥ Battle Techniques For War-Weary Saints/<u>Book</u> (32pg/B-07/$5)

⑦ Seeds of Wisdom on Adversity/<u>Book</u> (32pg/B-21/$3)

DR. MIKE MURDOCK

The Wisdom Center
All 7 Books Only $30!
Retail Value $38
WBL-25
Wisdom Is The Principal Thing

Add 10% For S/H

Quantity Prices Available Upon Request

*This offer expires December 31, 2006. **Each Wisdom Book may be purchased separately if so desired.

THE WISDOM CENTER 1-888-WISDOM-1
4051 Denton Highway • Fort Worth, TX 76117   1-817-759-0300

Website:
TheWisdomCenter.tv

B

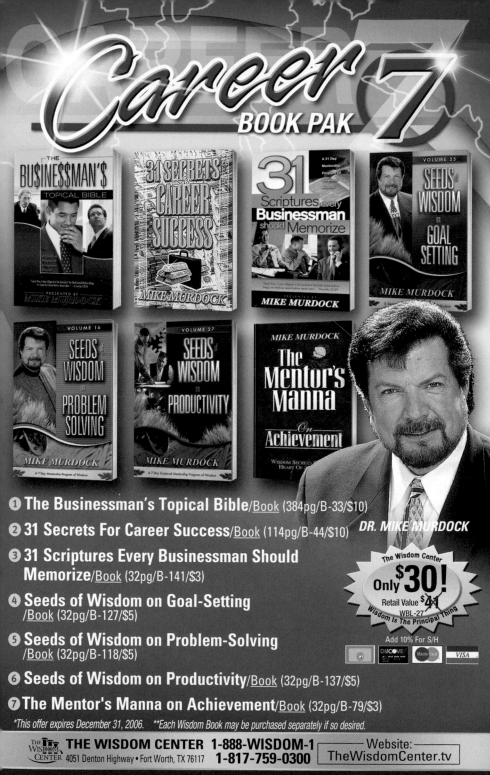

Career BOOK PAK 7

THE BUSINESSMAN'S TOPICAL BIBLE
PRESENTED BY MIKE MURDOCK

31 SECRETS FOR CAREER SUCCESS
MIKE MURDOCK

31 Scriptures every Businessman should Memorize
MIKE MURDOCK

SEEDS of WISDOM on GOAL SETTING VOLUME 25
MIKE MURDOCK

SEEDS of WISDOM on PROBLEM SOLVING VOLUME 16
MIKE MURDOCK

SEEDS of WISDOM on PRODUCTIVITY VOLUME 27
MIKE MURDOCK

MIKE MURDOCK The Mentor's Manna On Achievement

DR. MIKE MURDOCK

① **The Businessman's Topical Bible**/<u>Book</u> (384pg/B-33/$10)

② **31 Secrets For Career Success**/<u>Book</u> (114pg/B-44/$10)

③ **31 Scriptures Every Businessman Should Memorize**/<u>Book</u> (32pg/B-141/$3)

④ **Seeds of Wisdom on Goal-Setting** /<u>Book</u> (32pg/B-127/$5)

⑤ **Seeds of Wisdom on Problem-Solving** /<u>Book</u> (32pg/B-118/$5)

⑥ **Seeds of Wisdom on Productivity**/<u>Book</u> (32pg/B-137/$5)

⑦ **The Mentor's Manna on Achievement**/<u>Book</u> (32pg/B-79/$3)

The Wisdom Center
Only **$30!**
Retail Value $41
WBL-27
Wisdom Is The Principal Thing

Add 10% For S/H

*This offer expires December 31, 2006. **Each Wisdom Book may be purchased separately if so desired.*

D

The Million

THE UNCOMMON MILLIONAIRE $UCCE$$ SYSTEM (Series 1-3) 📀

Money is a tool to produce and create good things for other people.

Throughout the Scriptures, God has always promised Uncommon Financial Provision for those who are obedient to His laws and statutes (Deuteronomy 28:1-14/Psalm 112:1-3).

Years ago, an anointing swept over me while I was in prayer in The Secret Place here in my home where I have lived for the past 25 years. While praying, I envisioned 300 Christian Business People kneeling in the presence of God. They were seeking a divine Mantle of Prosperity and Favor to come upon their life. Their heart's goal was for anointed hands for Uncommon Productivity that would unleash *financial* blessing. I asked The Holy Spirit to pour divine Wisdom through my mind, my mouth and my ministry...and raise up **300 Problem-Solvers** who would become Millionaires for the Cause of Christ. I call them Uncommon Millionaires...because they would give God the glory, the praise and all the honor and stay humble and obedient to the mentorship voice of The Holy Spirit.

Pray about joining **The Millionaire 300**...and sowing a special Seed of $300 into this work and vision.

My special Gift to celebrate your membership and Seed is The Uncommon Millionaire Success System.

Mike

Are You Drowning In A Sea Of Debt? Receive an unforgettable impartation of Secrets of Financial Mentorship from proven Financial Achievers and Uncommon Millionaires who have studied the Laws of Blessing.

Do You Dream of Being An Uncommon Millionaire? The steps to becoming a Millionaire will surprise you...it is not what you think! Be ready to receive the rewards of your faith.

Accurately Applied These Truths Can Set You On The Path You Never Before Dreamed Possible.
You Will Learn...
▸ Wise Investment Techniques Used By Uncommon Millionaires
▸ The Three Steps To A Debt-Free Lifestyle
▸ What To Do When You Face A Tax or Credit Crisis
▸ What To Do When You Have Made A Major Financial Mistake
▸ Five Keys To Making Financial Decisions
▸ How To Get Out of Debt And Become An Uncommon Financial Champion For The Kingdom of God
▸ Tips on Estate Planning
▸ How To Rebuild Your Credit When You Have Made Great Mistakes
▸ The Hidden Secrets To Managing Your Time Effectively
▸ What To Do When You Have Made A Major Financial Mistake
▸ Five Keys To Effective Negotiation

18 LIVE Mentorship Sessions!   ***Cannot Be Purchased.**

aire 300

A 3 Volume Set Which Contains 6 Sessions Each, A Total Of 18 Sessions.

SERIES 1

The Uncommon Millionaire $uccess $ystem

MIKE MURDOCK

SERIES 2

The Uncommon Millionaire $uccess $ystem

MIKE MURDOCK

The Uncommon Millionaire $uccess $ystem

MURDOCK

*Cannot Be Purchased.

THE WISDOM CENTER
4051 Denton Highway • Fort Worth, TX 76117
1-888-WISDOM-1
1-817-759-0300
— Website: —
TheWisdomCenter.tv

G

The CRISIS COLLECTION

You Get All 6 For One Great Price!

1. **7 Keys For Surviving A Crisis**/DVD (MMPL-04D/$10)
2. **You Can Make It!**/Music CD (MMML-05/$10)
3. **Wisdom For Crisis Times**/6 Cassettes (TS-40/$30)
4. **Seeds of Wisdom on Overcoming**/Book (32pg/B-17/$3)
5. **Seeds of Wisdom on Motivating Yourself**/Book (32pg/B-171/$5)
6. **Wisdom For Crisis Times**/Book (112pg/B-40/$9)

Also Included... Two Free Bonus Books!

*This offer expires December 31, 2006.   **Each Wisdom Product may be purchased separately if so desired.

The Wisdom Center
Celebrating 40 Years of Global Ministry!
Wisdom Is The Principal Thing

The Wisdom Center
Only **$40**!
Retail Value $67
PAK-16
Wisdom Is The Principal Thing

Add 10% For S/H

H

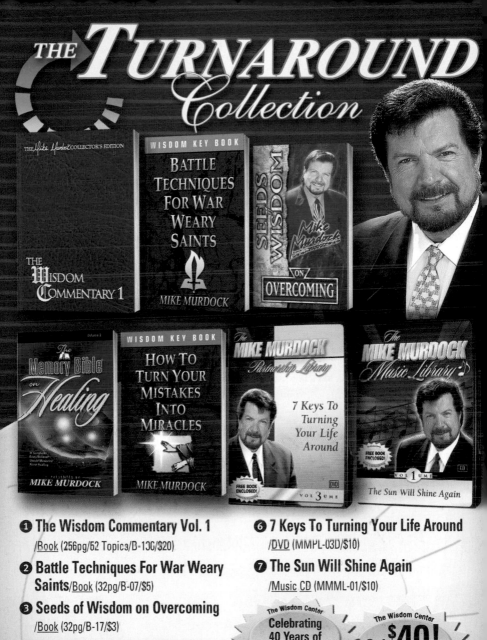

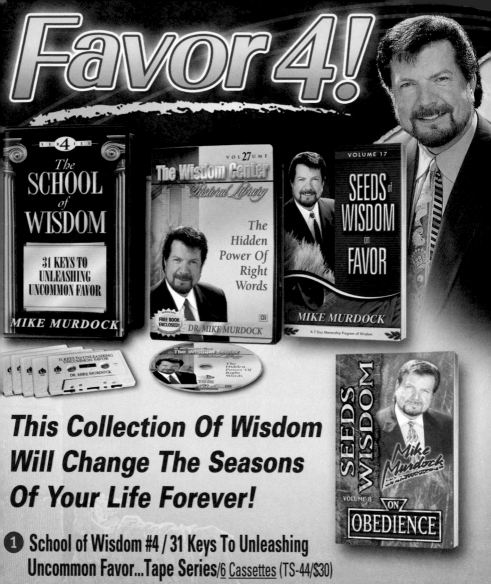

Favor 4!

The SCHOOL of WISDOM
SERIES 4
31 KEYS TO UNLEASHING UNCOMMON FAVOR
MIKE MURDOCK

The Wisdom Center
Pastoral Library
VOLUME 27
The Hidden Power Of Right Words
FREE BOOK ENCLOSED!
DR. MIKE MURDOCK

VOLUME 17
SEEDS of WISDOM on FAVOR
MIKE MURDOCK
A 7 Day Mentorship Program of Wisdom

SEEDS of WISDOM
Mike Murdock
VOLUME 8
on OBEDIENCE

This Collection Of Wisdom Will Change The Seasons Of Your Life Forever!

1 School of Wisdom #4 / 31 Keys To Unleashing Uncommon Favor...Tape Series/<u>6 Cassettes</u> (TS-44/$30)

2 The Hidden Power Of Right Words... *The Wisdom Center Pastoral Library*/<u>CD</u> (WCPL-27/$10)

3 Seeds of Wisdom on Favor/<u>Book</u> (32pg/B-119/$5)

4 Seeds of Wisdom on Obedience/<u>Book</u> (32pg/B-20/$3)

The Wisdom Center
Only **$35!**
Retail Value $48
Wisdom Is The Principal Thing
PAK-12

Add 10% For S/H

*This offer expires December 31, 2006.   **Each Wisdom Product may be purchased separately if so desired.*

THE WISDOM CENTER   1-888-WISDOM-1
4051 Denton Highway • Fort Worth, TX 76117   1-817-759-0300

Website:
TheWisdomCenter.tv

This Gift Of Appreciation Will Change Your Bible Study For The Rest Of Your Life.

The Wisdom Bible

MY GIFT OF APPRECIATION
Celebrating Your Sponsorship Seed of $1,000 For The Prayer Center & TV Studio Complex
B-235
Wisdom Is The Principal Thing

M

Spirit Music.

The Mike Murdock Music Library

LOVE SONGS TO THE HOLY SPIRIT
Written In The Secret Place

TS-59

THE HOLY SPIRIT HANDBOOK
What You Need To Know About Your Daily Companion, The Holy Spirit

LOVE SONGS TO THE HOLY SPIRIT
DR. MIKE MURDOCK

Songs...

1. A Holy Place
2. Anything You Want
3. Everything Comes From You
4. Fill This Place With Your Presence
5. First Thing Every Morning
6. Holy Spirit, I Want To Hear You
7. Holy Spirit, Move Again
8. Holy Spirit, You Are Enough
9. I Don't Know What I Would Do Without You
10. I Let Go (Of Anything That Stops Me)
11. I'll Just Fall On You
12. I Love You, Holy Spirit
13. I'm Building My Life Around You
14. I'm Giving Myself To You
15. I'm In Love! I'm In Love!
16. I Need Water (Holy Spirit, You're My Well)
17. In The Secret Place

18. In Your Presence, I'm Always Changed
19. In Your Presence (Miracles Are Born)
20. I've Got To Live In Your Presence
21. I Want To Hear Your Voice
22. I Will Do Things Your Way
23. Just One Day At A Time
24. Meet Me In The Secret Place
25. More Than Ever Before
26. Nobody Else Does What You Do
27. No No Walls!
28. Nothing Else Matters Anymore (Since I've Been In The Presence Of You Lord)
29. Nowhere Else
30. Once Again You've Answered
31. Only A Fool Would Try (To Live Without You)
32. Take Me Now

33. Teach Me How To Please You
34. There's No Place I'd Rather Be
35. Thy Word Is All That Matters
36. When I Get In Your Presence
37. You're The Best Thing (That's Ever Happened To Me)
38. You Are Wonderful
39. You've Done It Once
40. You Keep Changing Me
41. You Satisfy

THE WISDOM CENTER 1-888-WISDOM-1
4051 Denton Highway • Fort Worth, TX 76117 1-817-759-0300
Website: TheWisdomCenter.tv

*This offer expires December 31, 2006. **Each Wisdom Product may be purchased separately if so desired.

Financial $ecrets.

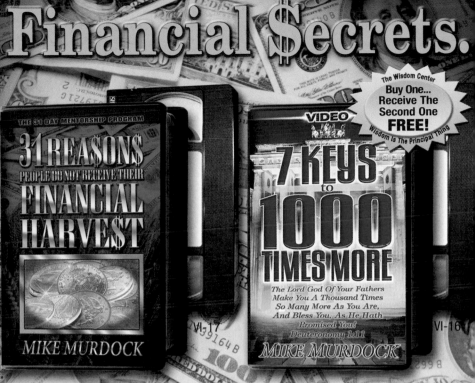

Your Financial World Will Change Forever.

▸ 8 Scriptural Reasons You Should Pursue Financial Prosperity

▸ The Secret Prayer Key You Need When Making A Financial Request To God

▸ The Weapon Of Expectation And The 5 Miracles It Unlocks

▸ How To Discern Those Who Qualify To Receive Your Financial Assistance

▸ How To Predict The Miracle Moment God Will Schedule Your Financial Breakthrough

▸ Habits Of Uncommon Achievers

▸ The Greatest Success Law I Ever Discovered

▸ How To Discern Your Place Of Assignment, The Only Place Financial Provision Is Guaranteed

▸ 3 Secret Keys In Solving Problems For Others

*This offer expires December 31, 2006.   **Each Wisdom Product may be purchased separately if so desired.*

THE
WISDOM BIBLE

Partnership Edition

Over 120 Wisdom Study Guides Included Such As:

- ▶ *10 Qualities Of Uncommon Achievers*
- ▶ *18 Facts You Should Know About The Anointing*
- ▶ *21 Facts To Help You Identify Those Assigned To You*
- ▶ *31 Facts You Should Know About Your Assignment*
- ▶ *8 Keys That Unlock Victory In Every Attack*
- ▶ *22 Defense Techniques To Remember During Seasons Of Personal Attack*
- ▶ *20 Wisdom Keys And Techniques To Remember During An Uncommon Battle*
- ▶ *11 Benefits You Can Expect From God*
- ▶ *31 Facts You Should Know About Favor*
- ▶ *The Covenant Of The 58 Blessings*
- ▶ *7 Keys To Receiving Your Miracle*
- ▶ *16 Facts You Should Remember About Contentious People*
- ▶ *5 Facts Solomon Taught About Contracts*
- ▶ *7 Facts You Should Know About Conflict*
- ▶ *6 Steps That Can Unlock Your Self-Confidence*
- ▶ *And Much More!*

Your **Partnership** makes such a difference in The Wisdom Center Outreach Ministries. I wanted to place a Gift in your hand that could last a **lifetime** for you and your family...**The Wisdom Study Bible.**

This Partnership Edition Bible contains 160 pages of my Personal Study Notes...that could forever change your Bible Study of The Word of God. This **Partnership Edition...**is my personal **Gift of Appreciation** when you sow your Sponsorship Seed of $1,000 to help us complete The Prayer Center and TV Studio Complex. An Uncommon Seed Always Creates An Uncommon Harvest!

Thank you from my heart for your Seed of Obedience (Luke 6:38). *Mike*

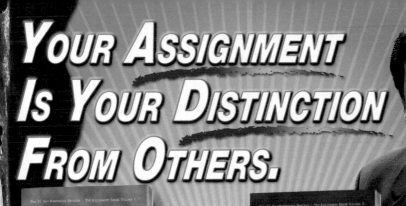

YOUR ASSIGNMENT IS YOUR DISTINCTION FROM OTHERS.

Uncommon Wisdom For Discovering Your Life Assignment.

❶ The Dream & The Destiny
Vol 1/<u>Book</u> (164 pg/B-74/$10)

❷ The Anointing & The Adversity
Vol 2/<u>Book</u> (192 pg/B-75/$10)

❸ The Trials & The Triumphs
Vol 3/<u>Book</u> (160 pg/B-97/$10)

❹ The Pain & The Passion
Vol 4/<u>Book</u> (144 pg/B-98/$10)

BOOK PAK

"Buy 3 Books & Get The 4th Book Free!"

The Wisdom Center
All 4 Books Only $30!
Retail Value $40
WBL-14
Wisdom Is The Principal Thing

Add 10% For S/H

THE WISDOM CENTER
4051 Denton Highway • Fort Worth, TX 76117

1-888-WISDOM-1
1-817-759-0300

Website:
TheWisdomCenter.tv

JOIN THE
Wisdom Key 3000
TODAY!

Dear Partner,

God has connected us!

I have asked the Holy Spirit for 3000 Special Partners who will plant a monthly Seed of $58.00 to help me bring the gospel around the world. (58 represents 58 kinds of blessings in the Bible.)

Will you become my monthly Faith Partner in The Wisdom Key 3000? Your monthly Seed of $58.00 is so powerful in helping heal broken lives. When you sow into the work of God, 4 Miracle Harvests are guaranteed in Scripture:

► Uncommon Protection (Mal. 3:10-11)
► Uncommon Favor (Lk. 6:38)
► Uncommon Health (Isa. 58:8)
► Financial Ideas and Wisdom (Deut. 8:18)

Your Faith Partner,

Mike Murdock

PP-03

☐ *Yes Mike, I want to join The Wisdom Key 3000. Please rush The Wisdom Key Partnership Pak to me today!*

☐ *Enclosed is my first monthly Seed-Faith Promise of:* ☐ $58 ☐ Other $_____.

☐ CHECK ☐ MONEY ORDER ☐ AMEX ☐ DISCOVER ☐ MASTERCARD ☐ VISA

Credit Card # _____ Exp. ____/____

Signature _____

Name _____ Birth Date ___/___/___

Address _____

City _____ State _____ Zip _____

Phone _____ E-Mail _____

Your Seed-Faith offerings are used to support The Wisdom Center and all its programs. Your transaction may be electronically deposited. The Wisdom Center reserves the right to redirect funds as needed in order to carry out our charitable purpose.

Clip and mail completed form to:

THE WISDOM CENTER 1-888-WISDOM-1
4051 Denton Highway • Fort Worth, TX 76117 **1-817-759-0300**

── Website: ──
TheWisdomCenter.tv

P